D1570123

New Atlantis

Begun by the

LORD VERULAM,

Viscount St. Alban's:

AND

Continued by R. H. ESQUIRE

New Atlantis

Begun by the

LORD VERULAM,

Viscount St. Alban's:

AND

Continued by R. H. ESQUIRE

FOREWORD

BY

MANLY P. HALL

THE PHILOSOPHICAL RESEARCH SOCIETY, INC.

Los Angeles, California

1985

ISBN NO. 0-89314-419-3
L.C. 85-16785

Copyright ® 1985
By the Philosophical Research Society, Inc.

All rights reserved.
No part of this book may be
reproduced in any form without
permission from the publisher.

Limited Edition of One Thousand
First Printing

Library of Congress Cataloging in Publication Data

Bacon, Francis, 1561-1626.
  New Atlantis.

  1. Utopias.   I. Haines, Richard, 1633-1685.   II. Title.
HX811 1660   335'.02   85-16785
ISBN 0-89314-419-3

Published by
THE PHILOSOPHICAL RESEARCH SOCIETY, INC.
3910 Los Feliz Boulevard, Los Angeles, CA 90027

Printed in the U.S.A.

CONTENTS

Franc Baconi
DE VERULAMIO
HISTORIA REGNI
HENRICI SEPTIMI
Angliæ Regis
OPUS VERE POLITICUM

LVG. BATAVOR.
Apud Franc. Hackium.
Anno 1642.

Cornelis v. Dalen sculp.

Emblematic frontispiece of the 1642 edition of Bacon's history of the reign of King Henry VII. The figure of fame or fate is shown holding aloft the *Great Salt*. This is an example of the reference to "a solid kind of heraldry," described by R. H. Esquire where wisdom is represented by a female figure holding a Salt. Fame is winged and stands upon a globe (the Globe Theatre?) turning a wheel ornamented with various symbols, including hats, coronets, and the imperial crown. The title of the book is displayed on a theatre curtain.

FOREWORD

In many respects the seventeenth century may be considered the beginning of the modern world. Powerful social and political forces were moving in the substratum of European culture. In 1614 the mysterious Brotherhood of the Rosy Cross proclaimed a universal reformation. Alchemy was emerging as a science of human regeneration and the astrologers were turning their attention toward those heavenly portents which signified rapid and enduring changes in mundane affairs. The Utopians were hard at work structuring a political commonwealth somewhat puritanical but closer to the hearts' desire of the public in general. The two class system of princes and paupers was becoming unbearable and the constant feuding between Church and State broke out in civil war which further disillusioned thoughtful persons.

Lord Bacon was certainly a moving spirit in the fields of politics, science, and industry. He revolted against the institutions of higher education, insisting that scholars had picked the bones of Aristotle until nothing of value remained. King James I was the patron of the new revision of the Holy Bible in 1611 and there is at least an enduring rumor that Lord Bacon was involved in this important labor. King James I, although not a paragon of the virtues, was

sympathetic with Bacon's dream of the advancement
and proficience of learning and even read some of
his Lordship's publications which he acknowledged
to be "beyond human understanding."

The revolt against Cromwell brought the
Royalist party back into power and Charles II was
enthroned as King in May 1660. His reign started
badly but improved with the passing of time and
in the last five years of his life he gained
immense popularity. In spite of his numerous
shortcomings Charles II was a patron of learning
and, among his first official acts, was the crea-
tion of the Royal Society of London. This body
was largely dedicated to the new learning as
proclaimed by Lord Bacon. During the reign of
Charles II there was a strong revival of interest
in alchemy, Rosicrucianism, and broad programs
bearing upon social and economic growth. The
seeds planted some fifty years earlier sprouted
and bore fruit, and the average Britisher found
living a more constructive experience.

In 1660 Thomas Sprat published his History
of the Royal Society of London with a laudatory
dedication to the king and numerous references to
the debt which the Society owed to Lord Bacon.
The Utopian dream of a philosophic commonwealth
seemed near fulfillment and the king was inclined
to favor the project.

Bacon's Utopia was published in 1627 under the title The New Atlantis and was appended to a larger work, the Sylva Sylvarum or The Natural History of Winds. Bacon's secretary, Dr. Rawley, described The New Atlantis as a work unfinished because his Lordship's attentions were called to more serious matters. The Utopian idea seems to have gained ground as the result of the explorations of those navigators who brought home the first accounts of the civilizations of the Western Hemisphere. It was evident that the Aztec, Maya, and Inca forms of government had strong democratic elements. They were highly socialized states, comparatively free from the tragedies which had burdened Europe for ages. When Pizarro asked the Inca how criminals were punished in Peru he replied that he could not answer the question because there were no criminals. Bacon's New Atlantis describes the adventures of seamen who departed from Peru and he may well have been influenced by the glowing accounts of the great cities of Central and South America.

R. W. Gibson in his book entitled FRANCIS BACON, A Bibliography of His Works of Baconiana to the Year 1750, Oxford: Scrivener Press, 1950, under entry No. 417 gives a full collation of this work as follows:

"New Atlantis| Begun by the| LORD VERULAM,| Viscount St. Albans:| and| Continued by R. H. Esquire.| Wherein is Set forth| A PLATFORM| of|

Monarchical Government.| With| A Pleasant
intermixture of divers rare Inventions,| and
wholsome Customs, fit to be introduced| into
all kingdoms, states, and| Common-wealths.| [2
1. Lat. Quotn.| rule] LONDON,| Printed for John
Crooke at the Signe of the Ship in| St. Paul's
Church-yard. 1660."

In his more detailed collation Wilson also
notes that in several instances page numbers are
transposed, a peculiarity present in a number of
volumes which are now suspected to contain ci-
phers or special meanings.

This notes misnumbering, "Collation: 53,
54f. 54, 55; 62, 63f. 58, 59; 57, 58f. 62, 63;
pp. 78, 79 transposed."

For the convenience of the contemporary
reader, spelling and punctuation have been moder-
nized in this edition, but no major words have
been changed. The original title page appears as
a frontispiece, and the original first dedication
page to the King precedes the first page of the
dedication. The mispaginated and transposed
leaves are reproduced in facsimile from the first
edition of 1660, and are appended to the text for
the benefit of scholars. The Latin quotations
scattered through the book have been translated.

Gibson closes his listing with the following
observations:

"The first 6 pp. of the book proper contain an epitome of B.'s New Atlantis; then follows what is stated to be a continuation of the same. Archbp. Tenison described the above work as 'a great & hardy venture to finish a piece after Lord Verulam's pencil.'

"The identity of 'R. H. Esquire' is not known, though Hazlitt states that the book was written 'perhaps by Richard Haines'."

Directly following the title is an extravagant encomium to King Charles II; it would probably have highly amused the King if he ever read its glowing lines. It would not follow that this dedicatory preface reveals so much the opinions of the author as his anxieties. R. H. Esquire must have realized that Bacon's concept of a commonwealth was not entirely compatible with the policies of the English State. He hoped, no doubt, that his tribute to the monarchy would protect him from any royal displeasure that might be dangerous to himself. The dedication extends to six pages and the anonymous author proclaims himself as "Your Majesty's most faithful and most humbly devoted servant in the strictest ties of duty and allegiance."

This is followed by a poem in Latin honoring Lord Bacon extending somewhat over one page signed by G. Herbert.

A rather extensive preface follows; the general tone of which combines apology and self-justification. There is emphasis upon the moral responsibilities of government and the enlargement of knowledge throughout the kingdom. The author makes much of good laws and gives a number of classical examples with occasional pertinent quotations. Beginning on page one is a summary of Lord Bacon's New Atlantis. It tells that a ship sailing from Peru for China by the South Sea becomes windbound until its crew faced starvation. By the light of God's mercy, however, they reached a beautiful island peopled by noble Christians. After some delays the physical needs of the crew were cared for and they were told that the place was named the Island of Bensalem. Here was instituted the order or society called "Solomon's House," which Bacon describes as the noblest foundation that was ever upon the earth. It was dedicated to the study of the works and teachings of God and sometimes entitled the College of the Six Days Work.

Bacon in his original text set forth many details about the wonderful research facilities and the museum of arts and skills which had been assembled in the College of the Six Days Work. In the midst of this description Lord Bacon's fable ends and R. H. Esquire attempts to continue the narration. It is interesting that Plato's description of old Atlantis was also left unfinished.

It is difficult to avoid the implication that the College of the Six Days Work is a veiled account of an actual secret society-- an island of learned men in a sea of ignorance. As we continue to explore the text it also becomes apparent that the Royal Society of London was dedicated to the same purposes as Solomon's House on the Island of Bensalem where dwelt the "sons of peace."

In 1662, John Heydon, generally listed among seventeenth century writers on Rosicrucianism, published an extensive and curious work called The Holy Guide. He prefaces this book with an almost verbatim reprint of Bacon's New Atlantis, but does not credit the original author. Heydon inserts direct references to the Rosicrucians at appropriate points in the original text, wishing to convey the impression that the masters of Solomon's House were Rosicrucian adepts. In the same volume Heydon describes the Rosicrucians as a divine society inhabiting the suburbs of heaven and officers of the Generalissimo of the World. As it is inconceivable that the identity of the true author would not be known to most of his readers, it can only be assumed that Heydon's purpose was to tie Bacon's fable directly with the Fraternity of the Rosy Cross. He must also have known of the supplement by R. H. Esquire, but he makes no reference to it. Not only these publications but many others, of slightly earlier date, present the concept of a secret empire of

the learned --its domains extending beyond all
national boundaries actually existed and were in
great measure responsible for a new awakening of
social consciousness.

R. H. Esquire in what he calls his "novel"
describes a new kind of peerage by which the
people of Bensalem, if truly qualified, were
elevated and duly honored. They were given economic advantage for their contributions to the
common good but wore certain insignia considered
more valuable than any temporal distinctions.

Sir Edwin Durning-Lawrence, in his most
intriguing book, Bacon Is Shake-speare, devotes
some attention to R. H. Esquire and what he calls
"a solid kind of heraldry." Durning-Lawrence
feels that the heraldic devices referred to are
found on the title pages and frontispieces of
books which may be characterized broadly as Baco-
nian works. Examples of them can be found extending from the Elizabethan period almost up to the
present date. Durning-Lawrence then reproduces
the title page of Bacon's History of Henry VII,
printed in Holland in 1642, which shows a female
figure holding in her right hand the great Salt,
which in R. H. Esquire's list stands for wisdom.

R. H. Esquire adds that similar heraldic
symbols of pre-eminence are assigned to the degrees for the clergy but he does not detail them.
Through such distinctions young persons are

encouraged to advance in learning and thus gain proper preferences and dignities. No one is advanced by money or favor but by eminent deserts. It is understandable that King Charles would not give wholehearted approval to such a concept of peerage and the author hoped to soften the blow by his elaborate dedication.

Remembering that the Royal Society was originally named Minerva's Musuem, there is a description of a ritual in which Minerva is introduced. The pages describing this ceremony are badly mispaginated which in writing of this type indicates the need of special attention by the reader. The hero of this occasion is named Verdugo and he is described as dressed in grass green satin with a cloak of the same color. He is met at the entrance to the sanctuary by a fair youth impersonating Minerva, the Goddess of Invention, and was embraced by the "Father." An orator proclaimed the merits of Verdugo's invention whereupon the "Father" of Solomon's House removed Verdugo's cloak and invested him with the long robe of Minerva and the one personifying the goddess placed on his head a garland overstudded with precious stones. Minerva then presented him with a baton and later he was led into a large room, the "Father" accompanying him on the left hand and Minerva on the right. After the ceremony Verdugo's name and surname, his place of birth, and his invention were duly registered to be preserved for all posterity in Solomon's House.

In addition to all such wonders there were
special areas set aside for advancement of agriculture and a beautiful arboretum devoted to all
manner of rare and useful plants. There was also
a section for the advancement of music, another
for art and a third for scientific pursuits where
rare, ancient telescopes and microscopes were
available. The Hall of Fame included many celebrated names and others less known who lived in
remote times. Prominent among the displays was a
magnificent obelisk on the surfaces of which were
carved the effigies of all the kings of the
Island of Bensalem. In the Court of Virtue were
brazen statues of the twelve apostles and monuments symbolizing their martyrdoms. In the Court
of Orpheus was a spacious fountain wherein was a
likeness of Orpheus playing upon his harp, and
the waters artificially resounded his harmonies
to approaching nymphs.

While some may doubt the source of this
continuation of Bacon's New Atlantis there is
much to indicate that it is a most significant
work. It certainly amplifies and continues much
of the spirit of Bacon's dream for the expansion
of human knowledge. This may have inspired Ash-
mole's elaborate collections of rare objects and
encouraged John Evelyn in his planning of gardens
and landscapes. The idea of a worldwide collection of significant books and art such as is now
assembled in the British Museum may have origi-
nated in Bacon's vision of Solomon's House. The

concept deals not only with the past and with the present, but projects the ideals of religious, philosophic, and scientific progress into the future. Although there are traces of early Protestant prejudices, the general tone of the work is highly constructive.

R. H. Esquire states definitely that Solomon's House was the gathering place of great wits and Bacon wrote on one occasion that he rang the bell that brought the wits together. His <u>The Instauratio Magna</u> was an effort to record all knowledge useful to mankind and dedicated the wisdom of the past to the service of the future. Bacon believed that the tripodium of learning rested firmly upon the threefold foundation of tradition, observation, and experimentation.

These were certainly the labors to which the mysterious sages of Bensalem were dedicated. Bacon was himself a faithful child of the Church of England. All his writings bear witness to the piety of his erudition. He recognized Deity as the Father of all works and that the wiser a man became the more dependent he was upon the wonders of faith. Bacon was not unaware of the shortcomings of his Church but believed that a combination of integrity and intelligence could restore the glory of kingdoms and bring grace of spirit to all useful labors making them fruitful for eternal good.

Manly P. Hall

New Atlantis.

Begun by the

LORD VERULAM,

Viscount St. *Albans* :

AND

Continued by R. H. Esquire.

wherein is set forth

A PLATFORM

O F

MONARCHICAL GOVERNMENT.

WITH

A Pleasant intermixture of divers rare Inventions,
and wholsom Customs, fit to be introduced
into all KINGDOMS, STATES, and
COMMON-WEALTHS.

——— *Nunquam Libertas gratior extat*
Quam sub Rege pio.

LONDON,
Printed for *John Crooke* at the Signe of the Ship in
St. *Pauls* Church-yard. 1660.

TO
My most Sacred Soveraign
Charles II,
King of Great *Britain*,
France, and *Ireland*, De-
fendour of the
Faith, &c.

Most Royal Sir,

Since the Sunset of that Glorious
Martyr your Father of ever
blessed memory, and Astræa's flight
with him to heaven, here hath been

NEW ATLANTIS

TO

My Most Sacred Sovereign
Charles II
King of Great <u>Britain</u>,
<u>France</u>, and <u>Ireland</u>,
Defender of the Faith, etc.

Most Royal Sir,

Since the Sunset of that glorious martyr, your father of ever-blessed memory, and ASTRAEA'S flight with him to heaven, here has been such an INTERREGNUM* of tyranny and oppression that all laws, both divine and humane, have lain dead, at least fast asleep amidst these alarms. Every ENTHUSIAST in this PAR-LE-BRA has done both in church and state (as when there was no king in Israel) what was right in his own eyes. But the brightness of Your Majesty, so happily now re-turned, we hope will scatter these mists and not only restore our laws to their pristine vigor, by restoring them to us and all of us to our own, but make religion, as well as justice, shine again in every corner of your kingdoms.

To contribute something towards this so much desired happiness, I have adventured to present Your Majesty with this my mite or slender essay of a strong, though but yet supposed, government. Where, if in the ensuing character of a puissant

* A period between two reigns.

1

and most accomplished monarch, all Your Majesty's princely virtues are not fully portrayed (for I am sensible the picture may seem drawn with too much shadow), I shall humbly beg your gracious pardon; this being only the first draft of that immense beauty a more deliberate hand perhaps could not have delineated in more lively colors. Thus did APELLES by the sudden and casual fall of his pencil add those elegancies to his admired VENUS, which (as he averred) his best art and judgment could not mend or parallel.

Your Majesty, in whose hand the sword of justice is, God be praised, again fixed, challenges this libation. And I were an unworthy son of my dear country, should I not endeavor with hers to promote the happiness of him that is FATHER of FATHERS since both interests are inseparable. And though no reprive may well be expected for what your high judgment condemns; yet to doubt of your pardon were to derogate from your royal candor.

Indeed, besides the necessity of imploring your patronage of this novel, to whom more properly could this ATLANTIC scheme of a well-composed government make its address than to yourself, the fountain of all law and chief LAWGIVERS in these your kingdoms? As you excel in the careful administration of justice mixed with clemency upon all offenders according to your renowned father's example, so you excel in his policy also, in desiring to make the hearts of your people your chief exchequer.

Yet though your transcendent clemency emboldens me to this presumption, am I not so opinionative of these my weak endeavors as to think them either worthy of Your Majesty's view or any way able to add to your royal judgment or heroic virtues? For rivers add little or nothing to the main, whither yet naturally they send their common tribute. It is my loyalty and gratitude then that instruct me to lay these few gleanings of wholesome laws and customs prostrate with myself at your sacred feet. And as I renounce all opinion of merit, so I beseech Your Majesty to believe that I offer these rivulets to the ocean of your royal goodness, only out of a desire to discharge the duty of a faithful subject.

Now, that you may really become our SOLOMONA, our second JUSTINIAN and GLORIOUS RESTORER of our almost-lost laws and liberties; to the reenthroning yourself in full glory, the reestablishment of our despised church, and to the advance of the public peace, welfare, and prosperity of all your faithful subjects, is the daily prayer of

> Your Majesty's most faithful
> and most humbly devoted servant
> in the strictest ties
> of duty and allegiance,
> R. H.

NEW ATLANTIS

In honor of the most illustrious D. D. Verulam, Viscount of St. Albans, Keeper of the Great Seal, after the great Instauration given by him.

Who finally is he? Indeed he does not stride with an ordinary countenance! You do not know him? You will hear. The commander of ideas, the Pontif of Truth, the master of Induction, and of Verulam; the sole master of things and not of things and not of mere methods, the evergreen of profundity and grace, the innermost prophet of Nature; Philosophy's treasurer, agent of experience and of observation, standard-bearer of Justice; emancipator of the sciences, which of old led orphans' lives, steward of light, one who puts gloom and idols to flight, colleague of the sun; square of certainty, matrix of wisdom, a literary Brutus stripping away the tyranny of authority, amazing arbiter of reason and common sense; one who makes the mind smooth again, a mental Atlas in the flesh, while the descendants of Alceus from Stagira succumb.* Noah's dove, which seeing no place for rest in the arts of old, prefers to return in

* Alceus: the name of Hercules when he was an infant.
   Stagira: celebrated as the birthplace of Aristotle

5

itself to the Ark of its mother. Auger of subtle-
ty, descendant of time born of mother Truth;
vessel of honey, sole priest of the world and of
souls, axe of errors, keen in myriad directions,
arising from within himself, charitable toward
others. O posterity, help me who am thoroughly
exhausted!

G. Herbert, public speaker
in the Academy of Canterbury

PREFACE

The legislative and the coercive power are the two hinges upon which the great machine of government turns. The scepter, which is the shepherd's leading staff, is the emblem of the first; the sword, which serves as a goad to the sheep when they will neither drive nor lead, is the emblem of the latter. The one dictates, the other commands; the first declares what should be done, the latter sees it executed. Impossible it is that man should live without submitting to some government.

For had every one been left his own lawmaker, to have been protected by his own single strength, as well as will, no man's person or propriety had been safe, and millions of mischiefs in that anarchy had succeeded.

Each man therefore, at first seeing a necessity of parting with his single power to unite with a stronger (for united force is stronger) resolved to resign that up to the conduct of some one more wise and expert champion, whose authority and interest he having once espoused, accounted whatsoever that cunning man, conning or cyning, since called king, acted, as done by himself. The supreme authority or diffused strength of a multitude, thus by mutual consent, or necessity rather, being fixed and vested in one person, they all acknowledged that one their shepherd or sovereign. And observable it is, that in most places the shepherd goes before his flock; only here in Britain by dissonant custom they follow it. However, this sovereign, foreseeing that without a coercive power he could not govern so great a multitude (for the shepherd must have his sling in one hand and sheephook in the other), began to establish laws: i.e., to set hedges and bounds to secure himself as well as them in their interests respectively.

It is necessary to acknowledge the laws invented by the fear of injustice. (Horace)

St. Augustine, writing of his City of God, concludes it impossible for that commonwealth to be happy where the mores allow the collapse, even though the walls are standing. Religion, it is true, is the tie, from binding together: that must lay the foundation, but wise men must forsee that ill manners undermine it not. Now as that religion which is most conformed to God's holy will revealed, is to be allowed only: so those humane laws that come nearest to just and honest, i.e. to the rule of right reason, consonant to that divine truth, are only to be established. It were to be wished indeed that men might live without any law, that is, that men would be so just that St. Paul's words might be verified now of us; the law is not made for a righteous man, but for the lawless and disobedient, etc. But such has ever been the frailty of human nature

(which is still more prone to evil than to good)
that there was a necessity of bridling that enormous disposition, and by severe discipline to
restrain and compel, where religion, conscience
and reason would not lead. Good laws and fences
were therefore made and set; but the irregular
inconstant people, not willing to be confined,
broke or plucked them up. Hence those tears.*
They after a time grew lawless and disobedient;
endeavoring to wrest that sword they had put into
their legislator's hand, and by sinister pretences to resume that liberty which they had parted
with before. You take too much upon you, says
mutinous Korab; we do not want this man to rule,
says another incendiary. And thus though there be
and ever were laws to punish murder, rebellion,
schism, theft, etc., in a few single persons that
cannot resist sovereign power, yet when by evil
example the contagion spreads, they then grow
masterless; then will becomes a law, treason,
reason; then liberty jostles prerogative, and
sometimes even thrusts it out of doors. By wholesome laws then so to regulate the enormous ambi-
tion of the noblesse, with the seditious gainsay-
ings of the ever-querulous people, that the whole
may be preserved without subdividing into factions or fractions, i.e., to govern securely; has
ever been the skill and artifice of political
prudence.

* A proverbial expression.

Look into all Commonwealths, and tell me
where any were ever happy till good laws had
first composed and united them: the multitude can
coalesce into the body of one people by no means
other than the laws. Livy. Moses gave the law to
the Hebrews; Zoraster, to the Bactrians; Menus,
Sesostris, and Amasis to the Egyptians. The Me-
dian and Persian laws for their irrevocability
are famous. All places and nations have been
conformed to laws, either made by one elected
ruler, or imposed by one supreme conquerer, or by
consent of the best, or of the whole people.
Athens and Sparta, after their several civil
combustions, began then only to flourish and
increase, when the first had taken laws from
Solon, the latter from Lycurgus. Then did the
Attic laws flourish when Solon had restored to
that commonwealth that peace and liberty which
lasted above 500 years after. Then did the Athen-
ians in this Halcyon age (as Herodotus attests)
bring some of their laws out of Egypt to complete
their own institutes. The like did the Romans
after them, when necessity forced them to regulate their city. For they sent their Decem-viri*
into Greece, who out of the Attic laws and others
made by Zaleucus amongst the Locrians, by Lycurgus amongst the Lacedaemonians, by Charondas
amongst the Thurians, by Phoroneus amongst the
Argives, and other chief Grecians whom they con-
sulted, extracted certain platforms of law and

* Board of ten commissioners (at Rome).

10

government, from whence those laws of the Twelve Tables Cicero so commends, were at last extracted and built up.

But to come nearer home, how many pious Lawgivers has this little island afforded? At first King Ina, and Offa, Ethelwulf, Alured the Great or Alfred, Edward the Elder, Ethelstan, Edwin, Edgar, Ethelred, Canutes, Edward the Confessor, most of which Bracton mentions to have been our lawmakers? And doubtless whilst the authority of their respective edicts flourished, much morality and civility dwelled in this kingdom. To the Saxon and Danish (by whom England was first conquered) the last conqueror added some of his Norman laws: out of all which, that which we still call the common law was compiled as being the common extract of them all. This Norman, I say, governed this sullen nation like himself a conqueror, with a rod of iron; retaining some of the old, but imposing more new laws. And though the people struggled under the weight of his new and heavy impositions, and petitioned him that the laws of Edward the Confessor might be restored, whereby they might be freed from extraordinary taxes, yet neither he nor his son Rufus that succeeded granted them that immunity. It is true Henry I (who summoned the first Parliament) and King Stephen (who both injuriously grasped the crown did to please the people, the first only promise, the latter release the Danegeld. Henry II was the first to give life to Magna

Charta, but yielded not so fully to it as to bind
his heirs to the concession. But the people having once tasted of the honey were loath to part
with the sweet; and shutting their eyes again,
soon compelled King John to confirm it at Runny-
mede, the which old laws of Edward, Henry III,
that unfortunate prince, did more fully confirm
and restore afterwards. But besides these grand
presidiary laws, thus extorted by the violence of
the commons, from these easy and unhappy princes,
we have had (not to name the general and particular customs, maxims, and statutes of the realm)
so many acts, ordinances, orders, resolves, etc.,
made of late in the compass of but one or two
lustrums*, that the cunningest picklock of the
law has work enough to enucleate the sense and
meaning of them. Amongst the Locrians whosoever
proposed a new law had a rope about his neck to
strangle him, in case it was found unprofitable,
and pleased not the people. But this overwise,
just and learned age has produced so many lawmakers, regulators, proposalmongers, reformists,
etc., that I may well ask here as once it was
upon the spreading increase of the English Jesuit
seminaries:

Who will give the rope which they have de-
served?

But I correct myself as well as them. For

* A period of five years.

though our laws generally are good and just, yet
according to Aristotle's rule, the laws are con-
stituted like universal things towards particular
things. In particular cases and circumstances
occurring after they were made (for all things
are not seen, at first glance) they may be, and
are sometimes very deficient. So that to correct
the rigor of a positive law (which cannot always
carry the same bias in every green, and from
every hand) here the equity or hopoinia of it,
which considers of the time, place, person, and
other comparative circumstances more fully, may
be useful: so as the Lesbian rule of equity be
not made to bow and incline to the rough stone;
for then as that prince of philosophers compares
it well, it proves but a very leaden rule. Thus,
then, upon just grounds, as Plato tells us, in
all commonwealths there ought to be some changes,
i.e., by repealing old and enacting new laws. But
then with this provision: the statesmen must
behave themselves like skillful musicians, those
who do not change the art of music, but its mode.
They may alter the tuning with as little noise as
may be, and that by little and little too, but
not leave the consort, or by cracking the strings
in stretching them too high, spoil the harmony.
It is a received maxim in politics that all law
and government should be fitted to the humor and
tempor of the climate and people. Now, in general, we may observe that all the northern people,
and particularly the British, have ever been more
jealous of their kings and less of their wives

13

than those of <u>France, Spain, Italy</u>, etc., seated
in the more temperate clime southward. But this
innate jealousy (which is the fiercest, most
secret, and therefore most dangerous passion),
being upon the least occasion or none at all
sometimes provoked, does but minister fuel, as in
all conjugal suspects, to its own flame and con-
sequent ruin. The <u>British</u> therefore I say (who of
all people pry into their king's actions with the
most jealous eyes of distrust) have by degrees so
lured <u>monarchy</u> from the perch, so framed, model-
led, and mixed their government, that it may now*
seem to partake of all three, i.e., of <u>monarchy</u>
in one king; of <u>aristocracy</u> in his council of
prelates and peers, who were called to debate and
advise; and a little of <u>democracy</u> in the convention of the Commons, though they were only at
first summoned to consent and yield obedience to
such things as the great Council of the Land
should ordain. So that in this martimonial union
(to which King <u>James</u> was pleased to compare it)
the king was and still is the head, or husband,
and therefore is and ought to be justly armed
with the sole power, will, and authority.

The gubernatorial power being then allowed
in all ages and places, except in a few sickly
and distempered <u>German</u> republics, to be safest

* <u>And but seem, for really it is not so, consult</u>
<u>S.R.F.'s discourse called the Anarchy of a Mixed</u>
<u>Monarchy</u>.

vested in one single person, both for speed and secrecy; besides it having been the first and ever since accounted the best form since the hatred of a state (which never pardons) is more mortal than the generous spleen of a monarchy. It remains only to be provided that the laws and rules be also few and good, by which this as well as any other form of government whatsoever must necessarily be upheld and maintained. But to preserve this particular structure to which, as most universal and safe, all prudent men must adhere, I shall use this method as most proper: first search out the wounds that monarchy has and may receive from home, and then apply the balsam. The persons that strike at the root of monarchy are principally these.

1. Criminals, who avoid the punishment of some crimes by them already committed, commit greater in stirring up others to participate of their offenses, that by a community of error it might seem justified.

2. Indigent persons, who having spent their own patrimonies riotously, live by rapine only, and take any occasion to disturb that government they know must correct them. These love to trouble the waters that they may best fish in them.

3. Ambitious men, whom a desire of graping power in your own hands excites to debase and divest him that has greater. For the bare desire

of riches, I am persuaded, was never the only motive to sedition: the covetous person being most neutral, and ever found to be most averse from, and fearful of, all turbulencies and insurrections.

4. Luxurious and half-witted persons (I may well join them), born to consume the fruits of the earth, who having lived long, plentifully, and sensually, foresee not the miseries of a civil war, nor discern the specious baits of the cunning subverters of religion and government. For such, under the glorious pretences of reforming religion, restoring liberty, and the like, engage these easy persons into their desperate designs.

5. Passionate men, such as by a private impulse of revenge, like that of Ravilliac that stabbed Henry the Great, at one blow strike at the head and root of government.

6. Schismatical men or hypocrites, who under the vizard of religion sound the trumpet of rebellion most. And this has been done by the Ecclesiastic Boanerges, chiefly out of your pulpits, the schmismatical non-conformists, who instead of preaching the gospel of peace have fomented divisions, both in church and state. But to omit other causes of sedition, it is the chiefest mark of prudence for a monarch to steer by, to observe by what sober rules of art and

cunning he may if not prevent, yet at least suspend such dire effects and fatal catastrophes.

To cure the first sort, the laws must be good, few, easy, and those duly executed without partiality.

To heal the second, trade and manufactures must be encouraged according to the example of the Massillians who admitted no person into their city that had not some trade to live by, and deserving persons only well rewarded. Thus plenty shall be introduced, and poverty (which only teaches and makes men do unworthy actions) shall be shut out of doors.

To cure the third rank, honors, preferments, and riches must be well and equally bestowed, that a few great persons be not too potent and consequently elated, nor the minor noblesse too scantly recompensed and countenanced and consequently made apt to repine and murmur.

The luxurious or luxuriant branches, like suckers which spoil the growth of trees, may best be pared off by decrying or severely inhibiting all superfluous expenses, either in diet, dicing, brothelling, or apparel. But without hellebore*, how to cure the mad, debauched, half-witted persons, they being so numerous, I know not, unless

* The Christmas Rose

a law were made that more of it should be planted
in each physic garden. Yet it is to be hoped that
time and experience (if the wiser men cannot by
precept and example) must only reduce such men to
a right understanding.

I should now discover how a prince should
avoid the darts of revenge and malice. But a-
gainst such rancor and sly poison, I know no such
antidote, no such guard, as his own virtue and
innocence.

I should in the last place discover the way
how to avoid the wounds of those that shoot your
arrows publicly in your pulpits; and that is,
either to turn the ear, or at the first glimpse
of them, before they draw the arrow too far, to
suppress them, i.e., not only not prefer or encourage them, but severely punish them.

But I leave the subterranean miners, supposing the groundwork monarchial government (as thus
laid) the most perfect and surest foundation to
build on; and by these artifices and countermin-
ings to be kept most safely from being undermined
and ruined. My present design is to point out
such wholesome laws as may make that government
most happy and flourishing.

(For here are no new ones introduced, such I
mean as were never heard of or used anywhere;
this being a collection or reviving of many

wholesome edicts and customs formerly used or
still in being, at least most of them in some
places or other of the world, and thought most
convenient jointly to uphold this or any other
monarchical island government.)

How far this endeavor is attempted the ensuing discourse made parallel to the Lord Bacon's
fiction (who being a wise man of great law and
learning also, proposed and framed his Atlantis
under a monarchical government) will make mani-
fest. And though that monarch of wit and judgment
would not be the legislator, yet he has given
such laws in learning and all natural philosophy
and such essays of policy that succeeding ages
will easily submit to his overruling empire.

Thus much therefore is said to satisfy the
reader only, least prima facie he should suspect
that the following frame of a commonwealth should
be squared according to the Lacedaemonian copy,
or those agrarian laws in Rome, or should smell
of Plato's community, revived by King Utepus, or
any later republican.

The imitator of that eminent person would in
the next place satisfy the moderate reader, that
he could not desert his method and design: which
was doubtless to have framed and moulded such a
scheme of laws as was most consonant to such a
happy monarchical government as he lived in, and
died under. But he may look on it as calculated

19

for the meridian of <u>Bensalem</u> only; and as but a mere fiction, airy speculation, or golden dream. For such golden things in this iron age we may rather wish then hope to see wholly effected.

A little he should now add to excuse this his presumption, for he is not ignorant what censure they incur who strive to imitate the most eminent. Yet the more noble the design is, the greater is the glory, he thinks, in effecting it; at least in the failure the less is the discredit. So <u>Phaeton's</u> boldness was not checked without its just eulogy —<u>Though</u> <u>possessing</u> <u>great</u> <u>daring,</u> <u>he</u> <u>is</u> <u>nevertheless</u> <u>destroyed.</u>

It is confessed by him since his wandering speculations led him to the <u>New</u> <u>Atlantis</u>, upon the view of so glorious a platform he was encouraged to enlarge it and to add one cubit more to that rare model of perfection, which that princely architect left unfinished and would better have perfected.

As in this bold superstructure he cannot raise his worth one story higher, so he hopes he shall not detract from it or lessen it in the copy, they being ever allowed to come short of their originals. All his aim is to imitate him whom he cannot identically parallel: it being honor enough to carry a torch behind so great a light that, when blown out by the envious blast

of malice, it may be reenlightened at his sacred
flames which never can be extinct.

His last advice (gentle reader), and which
he begs of you, is this: that you would be
pleased to enter at the gate of this building and
not scale in at the windows. First view the
groundwork itself which is substantial and then
ascending by the stairs you may better judge of
the upper rooms. The lower (if he may so term
them) of the Lord Chancellor Bacon's are, as in
all fabrics, more solid, firm and thickest wall-
ed, and so more defensive against the weather.
The upper you may find more slight, but more
lightsome, and consequently perhaps more delightful also. And there (if your leisure will permit)
look through this upper model also; that is, read
him over, for as it is said of the sea that it is
sweeter at bottom so perhaps you may find this,
the deeper you taste. This superstructure is only
that which he designed and thought to have composed, that is, a frame of laws or of the best
state or mold of a commonwealth (as Doctor Rawley
intimates, who knew his mind best) but was never
by him perfected. The reason he gives for it was
this, his Lordship foreseeing it would be a long
work, his desire of collecting the natural history diverted him, which (as he adds) he preferred
many degrees before it. Now because he intends
not to build a Solomon's porch before this Solomon's House, he will summarily discover his Lordship's noble design of erecting a College of

Light or <u>Solomon's</u> <u>House</u> (as he himself calls it)
for the advance of learning. And in case you
cannot find leisure to read his original (which
you may best do, it being at the end of his
natural history) he will then open the door while
you enter in farther into the college itself.

Good-bye and enjoy!   R. H.

Although more governors know the art, neverthe-
less they are a hindrance towards one another.
                                        --Bodin.

NEW ATLANTIS

THE ARGUMENT
OF THE
NEW ATLANTIS
As it was begun by the
LORD BACON

This fable of the New Atlantis devised by
that Atlas in learning, the Lord Bacon, first
tells us of a ship, which sailing from Peru for
China by the South Sea, became windbound and
consequently (their store of victuals being
spent) ready to famish. But the next day's dawn-
ing discovered the light of God's infinite mercy,
showing them an island into whose fair haven they
assayed to enter. Approaching near it, they were
at first warned off by an officer for fear of
infection; though afterwards received with all
humanity. For another person, of place and quality, who examined them first if they were Christians (to which they answered affirmatively),
offered then this oath, that if they would swear
that they were no pirates, nor had shed blood
lawfully or unlawfully within forty days past
they might have license to land; to which they
all readily protesting were conducted thereupon
to the Stranger's House where they found all
accomodations necessary for their sound as well
as their sick, who by their assistance were there
soon recovered. Three days being passed, the
governor of that house, being a Christian priest
by function, offers his service to them and tells
them that whereas before they had but short leave

of stay granted, now the state had given them
license to reside on land six weeks. This courteous offer they embrace with all imaginable joy
and thanks.

It tells us how the next day at a second
visit the governor informs them of the quality,
nature, and custom of that Island of Bensalem;
how it was first made Christian, and preserved
(as the old world was from the deluge) by an ark,
through the apostolical and miraculous evangelism
of St. Bartholomew.

The next day's conference relates how though
they lived remote and unknown to all other nations, yet they had knowledge of the languages,
books, and affairs of those that lie at farthest
distance. How the great Atlantis (which we call
America) abounded once in tall ships. How the
people of Peru through the South Sea and those of
Mexico through the Atlantic to the Mediterranean
Sea both in ten years space made two great expe-
ditions upon Bensalem; but by the valor of one
Altabin, King thereof, a wise and great warrior
(who cut off their land forces from their ships
and entoiled both their navies and camps with
greater force by sea and land) were repulsed and
dismissed by him when they were at his mercy.

How within one hundred years after divine
revenge overtook the proud enterprises of the
inhabitants of the great Atlantis, who were by a

particular deluge lost and utterly destroyed, some few wild <u>inhabitants</u> of the wood only escaped, which is the cause of the thin population of <u>America</u>, and of their rudeness and ignorance, they being a people younger than the rest of the world by a thousand years. How by this nearness their traffic was lost with the <u>Americas</u>, with whom formerly in regard of their means, they had most commerce. How, navigation decaying everwhere in respect of wars and revolution of times, intercourse from other nations also, by sailing to them, had long since ceased. How, notwithstanding this, there reigned in this <u>island</u> about 1900 years ago, a king whose name was <u>Solomona</u>, whose large heart was wholly bent to make this kingdom and people happy, and therefore is esteemed the lawgiver of the nation. How he seeing the fertility of the soil, and how plentifully it might subsist of itself, amongst other of his fundamental laws ordained the <u>interdicts</u> and prohibitions touching entrance of strangers, which at that time (though it was after the calamity of <u>America</u>) was frequent, doubting novelties and commixture of manners. How he yet still preferred humanity in all points, in providing for the relief of all distressed strangers. How that king, desirous to join humanity and policy together, and thinking it against humanity to detain strangers there against their wills, and against policy that they should return and discover their knowledge of that estate, took this course, ordaining that of the strangers that should be permitted to land as many (at all times) might depart as would. But as many as would stay, should have very good conditions and means to live from the state.

How the same king erected and instituted the order or society called Solomon's House; the noblest foundation that ever was upon the Earth and the lantern of that kingdom; it being dedicated to the study of the works and creatures of God, and sometimes entitled the College of the Six Days Works.

How, though the king had interdicted navigation to all his people into any part out of his own dominions, yet he made this ordinance: that every twelve years, in two ships appointed to several voyages, in either of them there should be a mission of three of the fellows or brethren of Solomon's House, whose errand was only to give them knowledge of the affairs and state of those countries to which they were designated. And especially of the sciences, arts, manufactures, and inventions of the world; and withal to bring unto them books, instruments, and patterns in every kind; that the ships, after they had landed the brethren, should return; and that the brethren should stay abroad till the new mission, with many circumstances of the practice in their places of rendezvous, and passing undiscovered in foreign parts.

It farther exhibits the most natural, pious, and reverend custom used there, of the Feast of the Family. It being granted to the tirsan or father of the family that shall see thirty persons descended from his body alive together, and all above three years old, to make this feast which is done at the charge of the state with many decent ceremonies. It farther relates how one of the strangers' company fell acquainted with one Joabin, a Jew and merchant of that city. How they have some stirps [families] of Jews who, contrary to all others, give unto our Savior many high attributes, calling him the Milky Way, the Eliah of the Messiah, and love the nation of Bensalem extremely. For example, how this man, though circumcised, would acknowledge how Christ was born of a virgin, and was more than a man, and would tell how God made him ruler of the Seraphims which guard his throne, etc.

It farther tells us this Jew's remarks upon marriage and their customs, all very rare and excellent. Also, how one of the Fathers of Solomon's House was entertained in that city in state. How the same Father, taking notice of the strangers being there, and sending Joabin to inform them of his intentions, admits them to his presence. And how at a private conference with one of the strangers he chose to unbosom himself, and spoke to him as follows in the Spanish tongue.

God bless thee, my son. I give thee the
greatest jewel I have. For I will impart unto
thee, for the love of God and men, a relation of
the true state of Solomon's House. I will keep
this order. First, I will set forth unto thee the
end of our Foundation. Secondly, the preparations
and instruments we have for our works. Thirdly,
the several employments and functions whereto our
fellows are assigned. And fourthly, the ordinances and rites which we observe.

Having thus at large (and therefore not here
to be repeated) exemplified to him each of these
particulars, with the true manner of their preparations and instruments, declaring unto him their
several experiments, artificial inventions, and
designs for farther discoveries, and making thor-
ough lights in nature, he, laying his right hand
on his head, blessed him, saying: God bless thee,
my son; and God bless this relation which I have
made. I give thee leave to publish it for the
good of other nations. For we here are in God's
bosom a land unknown. And so he left him, having
assigned a value of about two thousand ducats for
a bounty to him and his fellows. For as it concludes, they give great largesses where they come
upon all occasions.

Thus far the Lord Bacon.

NEW
ATLANTIS

THE SECOND PART

Obliged thus by so many extraordinary favors, or rather oppressed with the weight of
them, we thought we could not discourage our duty
of gratitude better than by a civil return of
thanks, accompanying them with a fair present of
the choicest things our ship afforded.

This resolved on, the next morning we appointed twelve persons to carry the same, fraught
with some of the richest wares and rarities we
had (each of them being well laden) and ordered
one principal spokesman with two other attendants
to conduct them and, with all our humble and
hearty thanks, to present it to the Father of
Solomon's House. When they came with it to his
palace (which was about two karans and a half off
in the next city, and built much after the fashion of that famous Escorial in Spain, though much
more spatious and beautiful), they found easy
entrance. For there the nobles need no porters,
none presuming to visit such places without urgent business there depending. Here, being entered into the anticamera, or great hall of the
second court, they eased themselves of their
burdens while the prolocutor inquired of some
young officers there sitting for the steward of
the house, whom immediately appearing, he ac-

quainted with his message, which was the tendure
of that small present, which with the general
thanks of all the obliged strangers they humbly
beseech that same Father, who the day before had
been so bountiful to them, to accept. To which
the steward smilingly replied: "Sirs, you are
welcome; but I can receive no gifts, nor any will
he. Yet I shall acquaint him with the occasion of
your coming," and so straightway informed the
same Father (who was busy in his study) that some
of the strangers were below attending his pleasure. All business set apart, immediately he came
to them, whereafter the prolocutor had made a
grateful acknowledgment of all his singular favors conferred on them, he humbly beseeched him
in the name of all the rest to accept of that
small present which as a testimony of their gratitude and pledge of their future services and
ready affections they had made bold to send him.
"What! pour water into the sea?" said he. "You
have not that rarity which we have not in great
abundance. Carry all back again," said he to as
many of his own officers, willing them to return
all again with the same hearty thanks, as if he
had accepted thereof, safely to the strangers.
And after a little reasoning with the prolocutor
why they should put themselves to that unneces-
sary charge and trouble, saying, that what he had
done was but the dispensing of public charity for
Christ's sake, who was only to reward it, he bid
his steward give each of the bearers twenty ducats apiece in new gold, in green silken network

purses (for he would not let them return empty),
himself giving the prolocutor and his two attendants golden chains of 200 crowns apiece in value; and at last, with much civility and thanks to
them all, as much as if he had received their
present, he courteously dismissed them.

In this ocean of plenty thus did we sail on
firm land, as if all the gold of Peru (whence we
so lately sailed) had been transplanted into this
Palestine. Amidst this abundance of all accomodations fit for the use of man, though we were
fully satisfied, yet we were as much unsatisfied
in point of kindnesses which we knew not in the
least measure how to retaliate or (if any from us
might have been accepted) such as would equal
those immense favors, so unexpectedly conferred
on pilgrims in that our languishing condition.
Thus, not being ashamed, but rather confounded at
the infinite mercy of God in casting us into this
Canaan, we sat down between admiration and joy
and blessed him, the giver of all good things,
conceiving ourselves no more sojourners now but
really the adopted sons and citizens of Bensalem,
and as it were in Heaven itself where no other
sacrifices were to be offered or accepted now
besides praise and thanksgiving. As we were thus
in contemplation of the divine providence, in
comes an alguazillan, or sergeant, attended with
other officers who had newly apprehended a man
that had taken up a purse with gold in it, who
having been discovered in the act of taking and

putting it up, and thereupon presently charged
with it, faintly denied it; but upon search it
was found about him and suspected to belong to
some of the strangers, some of them having passed
that way but just before. Therefore he civilly
told us, lest we might be affrighted or disturbed
at their coming, that he came to inform us only
how that wicked fellow thus brought thither had
offended justice in concealing and detaining a
purse of gold which they conceived of right belonged to some of our company. Thereupon he requested us to examine ourselves if any such thing
were missing, promising if we could justly challenge it, to restore it faithfully. Upon private
search, we found indeed that one of the bearers
having accidentally dropped it missed his purse,
but were very loath to charge the apprehended
party with it in regard of the severity of punishment which we understood by Joabin, the merchant Jew, was doubly inflicted on all such as
any ways offended the strangers. We therefore
resolved rather charitably to dissemble the loss,
saying we miss no such thing nor could we charge
that nor any other person with any such felonious
detention. The alcadorem, or judge, being in the
interim sent for and come (for there justice is
speedily executed as soon as the guilty is found
convict and sentenced) he proceeded likewise upon
their informations to make a farther and more
strict inquiry. A reverend old man he was and
discreet, and as gravely attired. His gown was of
fine purple cloth, of somewhat wide sleeves,

turned up with white satin, having a tippet of
scarlet sarsenet round his neck and down to the
ground before. On his head he wore a black and
white linen equally interwoven, and much after
the fashion on the top of a miter, having on each
side thereof a red cross, his hoary hairs appearing in curls somewhat long underneath it. The
alcaldorem, notwithstanding our partial and modest dissembling of the matter, upon some jealousy
of his that the man was really guilty and that we
were inclined to favor the accused party, desired
to see some one of those purses (which he was it
seems informed the Father of Solomon's House had
that morning distributed amongst some of us). One
of them we brought him, together with the 20
ducats in it just as it was given. Whereupon
comparing them, though he found the purses both
alike, of the same fashion, shape and color, and
the ducats in them of the same number, stamp, and
newness, yet because the party should not suffer
upon strong presumption only (since one thing
might be like another) he demanded of us how many
of those purses were dispensed to us. Here we
paused as not willing in truth to discover it to
the poor man's prejudice, and withal not well
knowing how to deny that truth which we knew he
could otherwise have searched out. We were therefore enforced ingeniously to confess that twelve
of them had been thus liberally bestowed on some
of us that very morning at the Father's palace.
"Then let me desire," said he, "each man of you
to whom they were given to produce his own, for

if you can show twelve of the like fashion besides this one in my hand, then may we be partly
satisfied that none of you are injured. For we
are strictly bound by the laws of hospitality to
protect all strangers from injury." At which
words we bowed in submission, but herein we
failed and could not produce any more than ele-
ven, the bearer whose it was then confessing that
in pulling forth his handkerchief by the way
homewards he possibly might have dropped his, but
would not positively affirm that was it. Whereupon the alcaldorem was not a little satisfied
and, turning about to us, not a little blamed the
uncharitable tenderness of our charity and indul-
gence in not readily witnessing against wicked
offenders. But because in the serenity of his
mild looks and gentle reproof appeared no real
anger, I took the boldness with all submissive
respect to palliate the offense and thus endeav-
ored to excuse it. That we did hope he would
interpret that their backwardness to accuse proceeded not from any the least intention to inter-
rupt their course of justice, but from a tender
loathness to do the least prejudice to any of
that land of charity where we had all received
such signal testimonies of favor and civility,
and such as we were ever bound to acknowledge. To
this the alcaldorem mildly replied, "As you are
strangers, your oversight is to be overseen, you
not knowing the customs and laws of this island,
where all concealers are looked on as accessories
and all injured persons are bound to prosecute

the suspected and in no ways to compound it. Take
here every one his own purse again and keep it in
God's name. And if hereafter you miss anything,
declare it and charge the party suspected immediately, for connivance makes thieves." At that
saying, the delinquent, seeing that purse also
redelivered by him to the right owner, confessed
his fact and humbly craved mercy for offering to
detain it. But all in vain he being forthwith
adjudged to stand in the pillory two hours right
against the strangers' house, and after he had
asked the offended party forgiveness and the
alcaldorem in offending justice, and all Christian people whom by his ill example he had likewise offended, (according to their custom) to be
from thence conveyed to the corringidoran's
house, there for three years to work for his
living, and ever after to wear the bell and
brazen collar. And though with much and earnest
solliciting often reiterated, we jointly besought
the alcaldorem to remit these punishments or at
least to mitigate the severity of them, yet he
would not by any entreaties be wrought upon to
remit either, but gravely replied that without
execution the law is but a dead letter, and that
impunity makes offenders incorrigible, and en-
courages others to offend also.

This said, with a grave austere countenance,
the alcaldorem sat him down, after taking me by
the right hand he had led me into an inner room

behind the Judgment Hall belonging to the strangers' house and willed me to sit down by him, the court and company being all dismissed. At which I bowed low and kissed the verge of his tippet (as Joabin had instructed me) and sat down by him. "Now, my good friend," said he, "since I understand that the Father of Solomon's House has given you his blessing, I shall open myself a little unto you also. And that you may not wonder at these proceedings or conceive we use overmuch severity, I shall satisfy you with the reason of this our law. It is only theft from strangers which we punish with death and the unjust dentention of their goods (which we conceive most inhumane) with this rigor as you see. Because the laws of hospitality we hold are to be preserved and kept inviolably. And though our laws are written in blood, yet are they composed of mercy and clemency. Theft among the natives here is but slightly punished, the thief being adjudged to be Adamist to that man he had robbed and injured till by his service he had made him double satisfaction; it being here but seldom committed. Though we know in your European countries the breach of that commandment is too frequent, and without any distinction of the injured persons severely punished. Here is no want amongst us, therefore when it is perpetrated we esteem the damage less, as the act is less malicious. For laws should be fitted to the temper and genius of the climate; each nation laboring with his peculiar national vices very suitable therefore was

that law made to the inbred disposition of the
English which there compels not criminals, as in
other nations, to confess by tortures. And the
reason is because that resolute people of that
island fear death so little, for should the tor-
ments of the civil law be offered there to an
innocent person he will by an obstinate silence
yield himself guilty or confess so in madness and
rather suffer present death than the lingering
pains which he counts as so many iterated deaths.
Yet, though this sin abound most amongst you, and
particularly in Britain, we conceive you are
there too severe rather in the grievous and capital punishment of petty larcenies where death is
so despised that the dread and frequent examples
terrify. For example, you suffer great men in
office first to rob, spoil, and oppress the common people, and when such depredators have made
them poor and in want, if they steal but a sheep
or the like (which they are often necessitated to
do to save themselves from starving) then you
either hang them, if the theft be above such a
value, or in some places send them to the mines
or galleys to enslave them more, and where
through extreme want and converse with one another they learn more roguery. Perhaps you banish
them, and therein you punish not them but strangers, every nation to a felon being his native
country where he can with most advantage and
least suspicion cease upon his prey. And thus
instead of tying up his hands you give his feet
liberty, sending him out with letters of

credence, as it were, with a pass to steal a-
fresh; or with Alexander's general commission
unneighborly to rob the world. We, on the contrary, where the offenses are not capital, are
much more mild to ourselves and less injurious to
others; causing only a collar of brass to be
clapped close and well riveted, that it cannot be
filed easily, about the offender's neck therein
inserting in Samian letters the quality and time
of the offense committed, hanging also a little
silver bell to it, that all honest people may
take notice where such miscreants come and have
warning of them. Now if any of these collared
miscreants file off their necklaces with intention to escape (for the attempt here is as much
as if the fact were done), not only he but the
smith that files it off is condemned to perpetual
servitude. These condemned persons are every
market-day brought forth into the marketplace,
there to be hired for small wages by the husbandmen to dig and delve till the next, and are ever
after called Adamists. This manner of punishment
we conceive better than the Athenian ostracism,
or your exile (none being permitted to go forth
of this island but a few every twelve years for
the traffic of learning and knowledge), and more
profitable than death, because in time such rotten members may become sound and be good subjects
again; and more ignominious than branding of
their foreheads, hands or shoulders; which marks,
being but skin-deep, in a very short time wear
out with the disgrace."

Here he made a stop, supposing me ready to
offer some reply, or start some new question, but
my ears were so chained to his lips that although
I was very desirous to hear him discourse farther
of the rare policy of their laws and government,
yet transported with wonder and abashed with
modesty, I could only answer with silence and
admiration. Perceiving my silence, or rather
wonder-stricken backwardness to offer any renew-
ing discourse, "My friend," said he, "I have
observed your great diligence in attention hith-
erto, therefore if you have any desire to know
more of our laws and customs (as all travelers
are thus delighted) it lies on your part to offer
the question; and I shall endeavor to satisfy you
so far as I may with safety to our state. For the
Arcana Imperii we dare not divulge; not for fear
of invasion (we being a people unknown in this
abyss of waters) but because it is a thing expressly prohibited by the first founder of our
laws." Encouraged with this friendly invitation,
as well as the occasion thus to my desires hinted, I thereupon assumed the boldness to ask him
whither their first Solomona was the only wise
founder of all their excellent laws. To which
query, as well pleased that I should move it in
his own sphere, he readily proceeded. "My good
friend," said he. "Since you inquire into our
laws most properly of me, who have been all my
life versed in the study and administration of
them, I shall let you first understand that our
laws (which are digested into ten small Codes, in

39

relation to Moses's Ten Commandments, and from
whence Justinian's have been partly since compiled) are the most just and perfect in the
world. They be not many, but those easy, plain,
and all written in our native language, and were
first framed by that same prudent Solomona, the
first lawgiver of this island; but have been
since revised and refined by that renowned Solomona Politicus, his fourteenth successor who
mixed them with the interweaving of some few
others, since Christianity was here first planted, extracting the best of all other nations with
a peculiar alloy of mercy and policy, and more
adapted to the ingenuous humor of this climate
and people. For we still add, expunge, alter, or
repeal as we see just and fitting reason. And to
this purpose, we have a grand seminary of students in the Law, erected by the same royal
founder, and since more largely endowed. Herein
are one hundred procuratorans, or Brethren of the
Seminary, who, as soon as graduated, ten of them
are elected by the alcaldorems, and sent forth by
those two ships which the Fathers of Solomon's
House embark their emissaries in. These, as the
rest for the traffic of learning, are sent into
all kingdoms and commonwealths, to discover what
laws, statutes, ordinances, customs, edicts are
there in force, and upon what reasons of state
established, or laid aside. Upon their return
(which is at the period of every twelve years) we
have half as many alcaldorems, twelve of the most
judicious of them residing in the same Seminary

constantly, and one out of every province, whose
business is chiefly upon the collection of all
their several observations, to make choice a-
mongst them, which laws or customs may be most
proper to the temper of this our Island of Bensalem. If we find any fit to be introduced (which
we seldom do, our own being already so exact) we
present them to the king then being, who if he
see cause enters it himself into the Codes with
the blood of a lamb or kid newly killed, and so
it is immediately promulgated and observed as a
fundamental law. This we think a quicker way than
by assembling the heads of the people's election,
since these many times, when convened, are either
factious or dilatory, especially when the sober
people conceive they are bound to consent and
submit to what the king and wise alcaldorems
think is fit and just to impose." Hereat I,
rising up humbly, craved leave to beg but one
question of him, which was how Solomona could
govern his people without a general convention of
his prelates, nobles, and heads of his people
since by their assistance and means in all other
Christian countries, not only laws are proposed,
but subsidies raised, and the public grievances
presented and redressed. To this he readily answered. "You may indeed a little wonder, since
custom with you is another law. But when you
understand the natural temper of this gentle
people, with the ground and reasons of their
tacit submissions you will believe they act wise-
ly; and may perhaps wonder why all other nations

move not so readily in their sphere of implicit faith and obedience. The people of Bensalem have it as a received maxim among them that their Solomona neither can or will do them any injury, they being the members of that body whereof he is the head. Thus confirmed they leave the management of all public affairs to him and his wise council, wholly submitting their lives and fortunes, whilst they follow their private vocations quietly, to his protection. This their modest result is grounded on this reason. The pilot that sits at the helm, they argue, can best steer the ship, especially when the rest of the mariners in their stations are carefully attending their particular duties, it being against the interest of a prince, as of a pilot, not to preserve his own people. Therefore, they conclude that the public utility, peace and security (which is the end all legislators aim at, and wherein their own is so necessarily included) are the chief impulsives to move him with the advice of his council to establish wholesome laws, in the due execution whereof (he being tied up to the same rules and forms he prescribes others) justice is preserved, and consequently the welfare both of prince and people. The truth is, in some kingdoms, as France, England, etc., and where the people are more dissident, jealous, and stubborn, the kings have been necessitated to call their subjects together, and that but of late years neither, to crave their assistance, else they could have raised no moneys. And yet in the first, by reason

of the frequent rebellions, partly animated and
fomented by those popular meetings, parliaments
of late have been looked on as fatal, and almost
sleighted; and in the latter it is doubted they
will not long continue, at least in that authen-
tic power and pretended privilege which they have
arrogantly assumed, if not too, magisterially
usurped. But to come to particulars, and our
particular form of government (which I know you
long more fully to be informed of, and is richly
worth your serious observation)." At which I
bowed to him with a pleasing, assenting countenance, intimating my earnest desires thereto, and
readiness of attention. He proceeded, saying: "I
shall in brief, my friend, delineate the platform
thereof, and then show you the elegant super-
structures with those wholesome constitutions and
general rules of policy by and upon which firm
basis all is raised and unanimously upheld.

"First then, we have a puissant monarch,
whose glorious empire by a continued uninterrupt-
ed succession has lineally descended to him from
the first renowned Solomona; most of that lineage
or, for want of issue, the next of the blood
having for these 1900 years worn this imperial
diadem without dispute or intermission. For we
conceive monarchy the nearest to perfection, that
is, to God, the wise Governor of the Universe,
and therefore best. Wherefore we proclaim him not
(as you Europeans out of ceremony do) he being
the known heir to the crown and immediate

successor upon the death of his predecessor. Only
he is soon after made sacred with the holy oil in
the principal cathedral, and crowned by the chief
archiepiscopan with a silver miter on his head,
and a crossier's staff put by him into his hand,
besides the being invested with the purple robe
of majesty, with many other decent ceremonies
peculiar to this our Island of Bensalem only. For
he is thus appareled both like a king and a
bishop as being a mixed person, and in both
functions alike supreme.

"We have many degrees of nobility, those of
the blood royal being eminently distinguished by
their great privileges and immunities from the
rest. The inferior noblesse are advanced by the
supreme authority for their extraordinary deserts
and not their demesnes, yet not exceeding a set
number, least they should divide into factions or
eclipse regal majesty. Nor are these their honors
always hereditary, because we esteem that grandee
or meaner person infamous that degenerates in
virtue or sinks in his partimony. Wherefore such
debauched persons and riotous spendthrifts only
are degraded as not worthy any more to be patri-
cians.

"We have a solid kind of heraldry, not made
specious with ostentatious pied coats and titular
achievements, which in Europe puzzle the tongue
as well as memory to blazon, and any fool may buy
and wear for his money. Here in each province is

a register to record the memorable acts, extraordinary qualities and worthy endowments of mind of
the more eminent <u>patricians</u>. Wherefore the <u>escut-
cheon</u> of <u>pretense</u> each noble person bears the
<u>hieroglyphic</u> of that virtue he is famous for,
e.g., if eminent for courage, the <u>lion</u>; if for
innocence, the white <u>lamb</u>; if for chastity, a
<u>turtle</u>; if for charity, the <u>suns</u> in his full
glory; if for temperance, a slender <u>virgin</u>, girt,
having a bridle in her mouth; if for justice, she
holds a <u>sword</u> in the right, and a <u>scales</u> in the
left hand; if for prudence, she holds a <u>lamp</u>; if
for meek simplicity, a <u>dove</u> in her right hand; if
for a discerning judgment, an <u>eagle</u>; if for hu-
mility, she is in <u>sable</u>, the head inclining and
the knees bowing; if for innocence, she holds a
<u>lily</u>; if for glory or victory, a <u>garland</u> of <u>bays</u>;
if for wisdom, she holds a <u>salt</u>*; if he excels in
physic, a <u>urinal</u>+; if in music, a <u>lute</u>; if in
poetry, a <u>scroll</u>; if in geometry, an <u>astrolabe</u>;
if in arithmetic, a <u>table</u> of <u>ciphers</u>; if in
grammar, an <u>alphabetical</u> <u>table</u>; if in mathematics, a <u>book</u>; if in dialectics, she holds a
<u>serpent</u> in either hand; and so of the rest;
<u>pretense</u> being ever parallel to his particular
excellency. And this is sent him cut in brass,

* An ornamental salt cellar as a charge on a
shield in heraldry.
+ In heraldry, a urinant, designating a dolphin
or other fish with head downward and tail erect.

and in colors, as he best fancies for the field;
only the hieroglyphic is always proper.

"We have the like degrees of preeminence
amongst the clergy. None are admitted into sacred
orders till thirty years of age; and then only
such as are well learned, and for their good
living also approved of first by the three universities and his particular archiepiscopan;
least the ignorance and frailties of the priest
should draw the function into contempt. Wherefore
our noble men's sons are encouraged to learning
and the ministry by our several great ecclesias-
tical preferments and dignities. To these they
are never advanced by money, favor, or marriage,
but by their eminent deserts. And that they may
not alienate their thoughts or divert them on
worldly affairs, only the chiefest of them are
permitted to intermeddle in the civil power and
publicly to advise when called thereto, or act in
secular or state affairs, least they should ne-
glect their spiritual. And for the same reason,
though they are not forbidden marriage, yet a
single and chaste life (in them especially) is
approved and recommended, they being by marriage
rendered uncapable of the best preferments. These
being the great faults of your European ecclesi-
astics, who either marry not at all but live
unchaste, or too soon get a wife, soon after a
living, increase in children, which care of maintaining them diverts their studies, spoils hospitality and, when they live leanly or leave

unprovided for, renders them and their profession contemptible.

"We have a loyal and peaceful populace, and no less virtuous, rich, wise, and valiant, who being emulous of honor and virtue, vie with each other in the service of the state. Nor are these plebians excluded from bearing either office or wearing honors when their industry or merits justly challenge them.

"We have a faithful, learned, judicious, and uncorrupt magistray, commissioned at the age of thirty and not before, for their deserts and not money, during the monarch's pleasure; though he seldom displaces any but for misdemeanors, and bribery particularly being so severely sentenced. For if any alcaldorem justicier, or officer judicial be suspected guilty of receiving any bribe or reward either before or after the cause is tried, he is forthwith suspended from office and after (if he is found convict) both his eyes are put out, being thus made to resemble Justice indeed which is or should be blind, and then from support; for all his goods are forfeited. While he that gives the bribe has his right hand bored through with a hot iron, and half his estate confiscated to the monarch, the other half to the treasury of charity.* The like justice we have for all simoniacal contracts, be it for money,

* Public treasury for the poor.

47

matrimony, or otherwise, where the patron besides his other mulet* loses his donation for ever, and the corruptor is for ever disabled from officiating in the ministry.

"We have no poor, no beggars, or idle vagrants; every tradesman and artificer being obliged to teach his children his own trade besides teaching them to read, to shoot flying, and to swim; the last of which, besides the benefit of saving themselves and causing good digestion, hardens them and inures them to strong labors.

"To this purpose we have in each city two large natatories, one for the males and the other for the females, about eight furlongs square, and some three yards deep in the midst to which it declines by degrees deeper. These are supplied with fresh rivers and delicate springs, and made more pleasant with swans, aviaries in little islands, artificial fountains and variety of fish, then was that famous natatory the Argrigentines made in honor of Gelon. In these we have twelve to preside as guides in their turns to teach all children the arts of swimming. These are called moisaicans from Moses, the child so miraculously preserved by swimming.

"We have likewise an arcubalistory in each city to teach all children the art of shooting

* A pecuniary fine.

flying with either gun, crossbow, or longbow,
which is the true cause," said he, "of all the
great plenty amongst us, every lad almost being
able to kill in half a day as much as shall last
him a whole week. If any man's child be ingenious, he is not forbidden to learn any other
trade, but at the age of twenty he is to choose
before the providorean which he will stick to,
and profess that only. Nay, the noblesse and
better sort are not exempt from labor, but for
the public good are brought up more or less to
some manual trade, partly to encourage others and
partly to gain themselves a subsistence when they
should fall to decay.

"We have every tenth child, or the most
ingenious and capable amongst them, chosen out
for learning and dedicated to the church. And
because some through old age, sickness, infirmi-
ty, weakness in body or mind become decrepit and
unable to learn such manual trades whereby they
might live, and others by God's immediate hand
through fire, lightning, shipwreck, maiming,
murrain* of cattle, death of parents, or by divers the like casualties be undone and left help-
less, we have in every city an treasury of charity or public thresory for the poor, maimed, and
afflicted, whence they are fed and sustained; and
a corrigidoran's house adjoining, to teach the

* A pestilence among cattle.

49

young poor orphans, and force those others to work that are idle and able.

We have in each city an episcopan or overseer of the clergy and laity in spiritual affairs; and an archiepiscopan or superintendent overseer of all the churches and spiritualities in each chief provincial city, all of them being subordinate in divine and civil affairs to our Grand Solomona. If any priest offend the civil power, he is first divested by the archiepiscopan of his function, and remitted to the civil magistrate for punishment; otherwise, he being consecrated to God, no lay hand may presume to touch or offer him any violence, be he never so vicious. If he offend in spirituals, he stands to the censure of the church only.

"We have in each of these cities a cathedral, taking its name from Christ, besides other twelve churches (which number every city has) taking their names from the twelve apostles: 1200. Parishioners or auditors, more or less, being apportioned to each pastoral congregation, and those forbidden to gad elsewhere, or have any subordinate lecturers to officiate under their proper pastors but in case of sickness only; and only such caretakers of souls set over them as the universities and peculiar archiepiscopan shall approve of. These churches are all built in fashion alike according to that stately fabric of your St. John Baptist's in Florence, in which church only (as there they also from us probably learned that discipline) the Sacrament of Baptism of all infants in each city is administered and no other; though they somewhat differ in bigness, architecture, imagery, and other rare curiosities. None of these have any churchyards adjoining to them, certain cemetaries being consecrated and set apart for the burial of the dead without the cities, or in the remotest places near the walls. We permit none to be interred in the church itself especially, those holy structures being raised for the living to serve God in, and not for the dead to sleep in, by whose stench also the living might be annoyed.

"We had an apostolical mission of twelve disciples also to reform all abuses in church government; but being fearful of innovation therein, and finding our own already perfect, and withal the many inconveniences, rebellions, schisms, innovations, and seditions, in all places fomented and raised since that spreading Jesuitical order had been erected, we desisted, and sent no more abroad. Only we have thereupon enacted many wholesome and strict laws for the keeping of these venemous and crafty perturbers out of this our island, least any of these evil seminary priests or seditious schismatics should sow their tares amongst our wheat, or seduce our peaceful and well united kingdom from those sound principles of religion and apostolical government in which it has stood unshaken ever since Christianity was here first planted.

"We have a clergy," he added, "very modest, but yet austere, serious, grave, and holy. These will not condemn or excommunicate any upon light causes or suggestions. Nor are they mercenary glozers* to sing <u>placebo</u> and sow pillows to their patron's ears, as too many within <u>Europe</u> do." To which I partly assenting rose up and desired (if he pleased to give me leave) to second that his animadversion+ with a passage I had lately observed in <u>France</u> between a priest and an advocate. "Go on in God's name," said he, "for I love to be confirmed." Then I told him how that in company at the chief city of that populous kingdom, which swarms with lawyers, a priest, perhaps upon some good ground, inveighed against the lawyers bitterly and concluded that had the devil a trial at bar he might soon find an advocate for money to plead his cause. "Marry," replied the advocate, "and could the devil die and should but leave a legacy of five pistols to any of the priests here to preach his funeral sermon, he should as soon find one that should commend him to the skies and carry him up to heaven again." "It is more than probable," said he, "but leaving them I shall proceed.

* Flatterers and smooth talkers.
+ Critical remark.

"We suffer none to marry till of ripe age: the man at the age of twenty-one, the woman at the age of eighteen complete; and those then to marry into their own rank, degree, and quality, but not into their own kindred till after three removes. We permit not the man to marry after his climacteric, nor the woman after the age of fifty-three. To this purpose we have registers in each parish to record their certain ages. Before they are asked in the church, their private consent of liking each other is thus notified. Each party to be married has two friends of each side to view the other party's body naked. This is done in the next natatory, the man's female friends viewing her in the female natatory and the woman's male friends viewing him in the male natatory. This is done to prevent dislikes and separations, for deformity of body not discovered till it be too late often breeds nonconformity of minds, while the same beforehand known prevents any after repentance or pretension of dislike.

"We judge it unfitting the woman after she know herself to be with child should let her husband carnally know her, or should so much as appear in public after her womb is visibly pregnant.

"We force not two young sinners to marry (though that obscenity seldom happens amongst us) as you too often do. For whereas you Europeans, when a servant is by chance taken in bed with his fellow maidservant, where perhaps the master had been before, unjustly force them whether they like, or will or no, to honest that wicked act by an after speedy intermarriage, so that the one being made desperate leaves her and turns rogue while she stays at home and plays the whore to both their ruins. We in this case only persuade them to marry; and if they will not, then we send the she-sinner to the corrigidoran's House for three years and the fornicator is adjudged to fast for twelve days and to wear the brazen collar as long. Nor is their natural issue, though they should after intermarry, to inherit, being unlawfully begotten before wedlock.

"We enjoin each mother to nurse her own child if she be able and healthy.

"We suffer no divorce but in case of adultery, which as well as murder, we punish with death, both in male and female offenders alike.

"We have here no law for a regicide, as Solon appointed none for that man that kills his father; because as he did, so do we conceive men cannot be so unnatural as to commit such nefandous* crimes, the killing of the Father of the Country being the highest parricide.

* Abominable

54

"We give little or no dowries, because fathers shall not necessitate or undo themselves giving large'sums as it were to be rid of their own children. The eldest male has a double portion, the females divide equally; and if before the age of eighteen the father does not see they are married, they may claim their portions and marry themselves. The woman relicit* is not permitted to marry again without special leave obtained of the archiepiscopan, and not then till after a whole year's mourning. For amongst the very Romans (where the wives would follow their dead husbands through the funeral flames) though such a one were too severely pronounced an adulteress, she who marries so many times does not marry, she is an adulteress by law, as if she cuckolded her former husband in his grave, yet here amongst Christians she will hardly ever be counted a saint, and loses some part of her dowry by a second marriage; whereas, if she can contain and live a single life, so much for so long, by the year, is added by her husband's friends. The widower may marry again without disgrace, but not till six months expire after his wife's decease.

"We expressly forbid all superfluous expenses (which would be better expended on the poor) by embalming, pompous funerals, or costly monuments to be raised after to preserve their

* Widow

55

memories because we account a good name to be the most lasting monument.

"We have fifteen provinces, into which our united kingdom is equally divided: these being by certain rivers, hills, walls, or roadways exactly bounded. We have in each province one _emporium_ (this next being one of the chiefest wherein the Society of _Solomon's_ House is erected) and six other lesser cities somewhat equally distant from it. In each city (which has its territory of equal circuit belonging to it) at certain days and hours twice a week, all provisions necessary for the use of man are to be sold.

"We permit not any markets or peddling fairs to be kept in any country town or village; for the first do but beggar cities, and the last only disgrace them and abuse the country in the vending of bad and unwarrantable merchandise.

"We have these cities situated upon the most navigable rivers, creeks, lakes or most convenient havens; all or most of them frontier to the sea for the better transport of our commodities from one part of our island to another, and those other adjacent islands belonging to this dominion. All [are] built with a bluish marble stone (of which here is great plenty) and those cut into spacious streets and even, as you see this city is. The houses are all uniform, well served with water, especially in their offices, which are always built half underground.

"We do not fortify our inland cities (which are but few), those only which are more maritime are munited* and built according to the newest model of regular fortification. They have not any suburbs adjoining, every such city having a citadel to command it and being strongly garrisoned; for our Solomona being so remote and unknown (though he fears not any foreign invasions, and less any civil insurrections) yet does he for exercise sake, as well to prevent the worst if either should chance to happen (we holding it unlawful to make any war but what is merely defensive) for the better safeguard of his kingdom, keeps always a standing militia at his own expense, without any tax or charge to the subject. Whereas you Europeans falsely suppose gunpowder to be the late invention of a monk, we learned the use of it from the Chinese many hundred years ago, amongst whom guns were in use when Bacchus made his expedition into India, which was about the time of the Israelites departure out of Egypt.

"We have all our cities built upon a little rise or ascent to them on all sides, both for the stately beauty and cleanliness. In the midst of each stands a large square marketplace which is

* Protected

environed on the one side with the prisons for
offenders, Corrigidoran's House, and the armories
wherein are kept the engines to quench fire, as
well as weapons of war, offensive and defensive,
great guns, trains of artillery, etc., all in a
strong and safe guarded arsenal. Right opposite
to these are the courts of justice, public halls
for all societies and companies, free schools,
and public schools (if it be a university) we
having three in three of the chiefest cities. To
make the others square, we have on one side the
theaters, common granaries, amoscadoes or lum-
bars, the bourse or exchange (if it be a provincial city) and the Artillery Gardens. And opposite to these the hospitals of all sorts, for old
and sick folks, for the maimed, for children,
orphans, and all that are lunatic. In the midst
of all which large square stands the Regimiento
or Common-Council House in each city, where the
richer and wiser inhabitants assemble to consult
of the politic government of the city.

"We have all offensive trades more apart
situated, as brewers, bakers, chandlers, butch-
ers, tanners, dyers, curriers, fellmongers, in
some back parts in the outskirts of the city, by
themselves, and near the river to carry their
filth away least their fulsome trades should with
the badness of their smells offend the more pleasant dwellings or cause infection. All forgemen,
as smith, metalmen, tinkers, pewterers, and all
other noisemaking artificers that deal in fire,

dwell in a convenient place wholly apart by themselves also for the better safety of the houses as to prevent the trouble of their impetuous noises. For this cause also ringing of bells more than for the calling of the people to church is everywhere inhibited. And for other trades and occupations, each has a several street or place by itself, as at <u>Algiers</u> in <u>Africa</u>. Thus though they resemble each other in many respects, yet in as many do they differ, either in largeness or elegance of building wherein they daily strive to excel each other.

"We appoint in every city two <u>justiciers</u> of the market (who are every year chosen) to make a strict enquiry into the just dealings of tradesmen that they make no ill wares or counterfeit. They are particularly to look to the water mills and other mills in each fortified city, and to all weights and measures which are to be allowed of by them. For if they agree not with the standard of the island, they are immediately broken, and half the delinquent's goods that fall by such false weights and measures are forthwith confiscated to the treasury of charity, and the party himself is sentenced to wear the brazen collar for one year or more, according to the greatness of his crime.

"We have in every provincial city a <u>Surveyor General</u> to set and order what reformation is best in all places adjacent and within his precinct in that province. As what <u>bridges, banks, fortifica-tions, aqueducts, conduits, channels, public works, inundations</u> by breaches near the sea may be prevented, as the other repaired and preserv-ed. All which publick works are maintained out of the common treasury raised out of that peculiar province, and <u>supervisors</u> annually elected in every city and village adjoining for that pur-pose.

"We have likewise a <u>Providoran</u> General in every provincial city whose business is to see that all the common granaries are always replen-ished and preserved; our corn being thus best kept from must* and the rats in boats upon the water.

"To this purpose we have in each of the universities a college for <u>agriculture</u> wherein the <u>florists, herbalists</u>, etc., study, examine and appoint what ground is fittest for corn, and of what sort, which for wood, grass, meadow, gardens, orchards, hops, vineyards, fish ponds; which for woad, flax, rape, hemp, etc., as also for all exotic herbs, roots, trees, and plants which will thrive alike here or in any country if ground fitting is found and prepared. These <u>prov-idorans</u> suffer not any commons (by which the richer that can best stock them thrive only) nor any wastes, bogs, forests, fens, marshes,

* Mold

deserts, heaths, or parks (but some few only for our Solomona's pleasure) but by enclosures or draining improve all to the best advantage for the public good, so that by these means the rates of corn, wood, coal, with divers other commodities, what scarcity so ever happens, never exceeds.

"We have many other good laws for the improvement of lands and woods; as first of all, that none shall cut down any timber tree but shall plant ten for it; that none of them shall be felled till of full growth, and that before they begin to decay. The landlord shall have a third part of the profit of all improvements, or at the expiration of his lease shall either give so many years purchase for improvement, or such quantity of the land so improved, as the providoran shall judge the tenant truly deserves. Every tenant shall plant all necessary fruit trees as apples, pears, damsons, prunes, mulberries, walnuts, cherries, chestnuts, etc., in all his hedges and places convenient, with which improvement only he may pay his rent and keep his family. The moiety of his pasture grounds [shall] be sowed always either with St. Foin, La Lucern, clover, or other as beneficial trefoils, and the other half ploughed and laid in for sheep pastures. They [shall] plant firs for masts, ashes, sallows, willows about their mansions, and osiers in all moist grounds: the first for firing, the last for use. All decayed farmhouses, barns, and

outhouses belonging to them [shall] be rebuilt by
the landlord, or the possession granted with the
profits for twenty years to him that will expend
the charge of building. No rich man [shall] engross all the commodities or forestall the markets; to which purpose each city has twelve Sitonans, that is, for every port one, whose care is
to see that none engross the corn by preemption;
but that the country people bring into the market
proportionally to what they sow, reserving only
what is necessary for their own families. These
Sitonans are all subservient to the grand providoran of the province. These providorans have a
power to summon all whom they please to suspect
before them once a year to give an account by
what trade or occupation they get their liveli-
hood. If such cannot give a good account, they
are sent immediately to the corrigidorans, who
either finds them work or lets them forth the
next market day either to the husbandmen or vine-
dressers.

"We appoint a certain size for the length of
all our swords throughout the island; allowing
none to be worn ordinarily by any, but some few
privileged persons in any of our cities.

"We allow no excess in attire of embroide-
ries or wearing gold or silver laces upon wearing
apparel; every noble man, magistrate, merchant,
or tradesman, with their wives respectively,
being distinguished with decent attire, suitable

to his calling or profession; and that fashion not to be altered.

"We have in the three universities, colleges (besides those for divinity, law, and philosophy) for mathematics, historians, poets, musicians, stage-players, alchemists, florists, herbalists, surgeons, anatomists, and physicians also. Unto the last are adjoining large physic gardens, theatres and schools. In all of them all the students are to apply themselves particularly unto that study and art they first undertake, and none other, that thus all experiments may be sooner reduced unto perfection, all arts and sciences soon learned; all these several colleges being very fairly endowed.

"We have one in the chief university called royal historiographer, who has a great pension allowed him for supervising all history that shall be put out. For if they do not set forth the truth exactly, clearly, faithfully, concisely and yet elegantly, without the least deviation from it: i.e., neither by omitting anything through ignorance, nor forgetfulness; his province it is to correct the history: that posterity may judge right of all preceding actions, and not be wronged by any sinister practices or false glosses.

"We have besides these in the Imperial City one eminent Academy of selected wits whose endeavors are to reform all errors in books, and then to license them; to purify our native language from barbarism or solecism, to the height of eloquence, by regulating the terms and phrases thereof into a constant use of the most significant words, proverbs, and phrases, and justly appropriating them either to the lofty, mean or comic style. These likewise translate the best authors, and render them in their genuine sense to us very perspicuous, and make dictionaries in all languages wherein the proper terms of art for every notion and thing in every trade, manufacture and science is genuinely rendered and with its derivation very perspicuous.

"We have also in each of the provincial cities (which have universities) free schools for the attaining of the languages, singing, dancing, fencing, riding, and writing, wither by brachugraphy, hieroglyphic, or an instrument we have made to write two copies at once, at one and the same motion, for dispatch. For all which we have public governors and masters fit each place respectively; chosen by the representative body of that academy every three years.

"We have likewise in every city public treasurers, aediles, quaesters, overseers of the poor pupil's and orphan's goods; who make a strict account every year of all receipts, disbursements, and expenses to the magistrate or governor of each respective city. These magistrates are

not elected out of the plebeians, tradesmen or
mechanics only, but out of the noblesse and gentry who are to reside in these cities, at such
times and seasons especially, we thinking it not
dishonorable for noble persons to govern in the
city as well as in the country. These are all to
give an account of their behavior and government
when their time expires.

"We have a law enjoining the chief landlords
equally and charitably to divide their lands and
tenements in every city and village, that one
tenant may not domineer over the other. These
tenures are apportioned and set out that the
tenants may the better improve their lands by
manure of all sorts, planting of trees and vineyards, draining, fencing, building, etc., and the
landlords to this end are appointed to let them
long leases at a rent certain without fine, to
free them for the future from the exaction of
griping patrons.

"We permit no usury but what is very moderate; and that but to some few virgins, widows, or
orphans who least know how to employ their moneys. Sometimes too, merchants or young tradesmen,
if they be allowed of by the chief magistrate as
not idle, prodigal, debauched, riotous spendthrifts, or not knowing how to make good use of
such moneys, and honestly to employ the same to
their advantage.

"We punish extortion severely with the fine of ten times as much as the principal, all which goes to the treasury of charity. But the party to the usurious contract shall not be a sufficient witness against the extortioner, because no man can be a witness in his own case. For such as hide their treasure, though such lose it as it were by not using it, yet if any one find it, it shall not be confiscated to the king, as with you it is in some places, but shall all be forfeited and brought into public treasury for the ways and public repairs.

"We imprison no bankrupts or debtors above two years, during which space (if he were reduced to poverty by his own willful negligence, riot, excess, or folly) if he cannot satisfy his creditors in that time, he is for his eternal disgrace enlarged; but sentenced to wear the brazen collar and silver bell, that all good people may have warning how they deal with him, till such time as he has fully satisfied all his creditors. As for decayed citizens, the richer landlords in city and country are ordered to receive and place them in farms (for copyholds we approve not of) or other convenient places and offices wherein they may thrive and restore.

"We punish all profane, atheistical, and customary swearers for half a year with the brazen collar also, and a pecuniary mulct to the treasury of charity for each offense. If the

party reform not in that time, the bell is added
also, that all good Christians may avoid his
company. If in a year's space he leave it not
off, his tongue is bored through with a hot iron.
The sacrilege loses both his hands and for that
his impious offense against God. He that bears
false witness, if convicted, loses his tongue; a
common liar his upper lip, and every malicious
slanderer his under lip. He that is convicted of
perjury has his tongue cut out. He that is drunk
once, is fined, if he practise it, he is interdicted all liquor but water for twelve months;
and so often as he offends, so often does he pay
a set mulct to the treasury of charity according
to the quality of the offender.

"We have a law inhibiting all foreign rank
Jews to live in this island, or any to have
converse or commerce with them whenever they land
till they be converted and baptized. And that
they may so be, we have a little island belonging
to us, assigned particularly for them, whither
they are immediately sent to be instructed in the
faith, and after they are converted and received
into the bosom of the Church, they are permitted
to live and trade here as well as those Jews we
already have (who are not so perverse as to deny
Christ) or any other natives. No kind of violence
is used to them or any contentious opinionist, so
as his erroneous opinions strike not at the root
of Christian religion, or they do not vehemently
inveigh against the professed truth, to promote

strife and division. But if they remain obstinate, or renege, denying our Savior, they are crucified in the same manner as they did our Savior. For we have a law, that if any foreign malefactor offend here capitally, he shall be punished according to the custom of that place wherein he was born, and every offender accidentally cast on this shore, or flying hither for refuge (which seldom here happens) we punish after the custom of the place the fact was committed in, as you do at Geneva, but if any native do commit murder on his fellow subject abroad, he shall not escape unpunished at his return, though the fact were done out of our dominion (which is a particular defect in your law of England) for in such cases neither time nor place should impede justice which reaches all.

We that are alcaldorems, before whom all suits and pleas are determined, as well civil as criminal, take a pledge of every one that is plaintiff, equal in value to the thing he contends for, or if he have not so much, as much as he can raise, which, in case he sue maliciously and wrongfully, he forfeits. In criminal cases the accuser (being under the Alguazillans restraint also) is punished with the same infliction that the accused, if he had been found convicted, should have been chastised with, if it appears on proof he maliciously and wrongfully have accused him. And here they are not hanged like dogs but beheaded or shot like men. These

upright alcaldorems not admitting any rhetorical
pleas, but short and simple narrations, chose the
dark that they might not be moved to compassion
by the sight of the malefactor, and give their
judgment without a word speaking; as the Areopa-
gites in Athens did, men famed for their gravity
and uprightness in judicature.

"We suffer no suit or plea to depend above
half a year, deciding it peremptorily without
farther appeals. If in that time they take it not
up themselves, or agree by arbitrators delegated
for that purpose, we free the defendant, and the
plaintiff forfeits his pledge immediately. All
officers and clerks, etc., in all courts have
their certain fees, and those very moderate, and
where they exact, all they have is forfeited.

"We have to prevent all fraud in sales,
mortgages, and conveyances of lands, certain es-
crivanans or notaries in every city who record
all such sales, mortgages, bonds, suretyships,
judgments, statutes, etc. Which book of record
written in Salamandrian paper, for a small fee
any purchaser or mortgage taker may at any time
search for his satisfaction. And for smaller
things (because we permit no private brokerage or
sale of movables to citizens or tradesmen) we
have in every city a great Amoscado or Lumbar,
where all goods are either bought outright or
pawned, to be redeemed in one year at certain
easy rates.

"We have no inns or cut-throat harbors (as you Europeans have) where the poor traveler pays a fine for his rest at the will of his unconscionable host. But instead of them we have strangers' houses, built and maintained at the public charge, in each of which honest governors are elected every three years who are to give to all stranger-passengers such fitting entertainment as they like and desire at certain easy rates. These are for the native strangers in their inland voyages; for the foreign, yours where you lodge, is only provided, and that without any paymaking.

"We ordain post-horses or mules, carioles, wagons, and coaches, which are to pass at certain days and hours their set stages, and convey them at certain easy rates; which is much for the better, safer, and easier transport of all passengers. We observe the like order for all water passages also, which we cut frequently between town and town for the better carrying of commodities. And to prevent lameness of horses, we erect at each Karan a smith's forge in all public roads.

"We condemn none to death unless the matter of fact be evidently proved, and by the verdict of twelve sworn men be so adjudged, and the party's own confession. In which case after he is found convicted by strong presumptions, he is to be kept close prisoner, and to be fed with nothing but bread and water till such time as he confesses the fact. After that, and that he has given good testimony of his serious repentance, he is according to the law executed, unless upon the judge's and jury's petition to our Solomona for his life, out of his abundant clemency he be by him pardoned, which rarely happens. All civil affairs of mine and thine are tried also by jury of the same number of able, honest, understanding persons, and such as are generally known and approved of for their integrity and understanding, these juries being never packed or made up from the ranks of the proletarians who many times with you serve for your money and not for conscience.

"We that are alcaldorems as well as all other public officers, when once come to the age of seventy, are freed from all public service and have our retirement sent from our Solomona, remitting us with thanks for our former services, and our former salaries still continued to us during life, to our ease and quiet.

"We have no reversions of offices, benefices or martial preferments granted; first, because our Solomona's liberty of advancing persons of known merit shall not be impeached. Secondly, least any attempt should be made against the present incubents lives; and lastly, that all persons may equally have encouragement to study and merit better in hope of advancement.

"We hold it sacrilegious to conceal, hide, or keep any goods from the true owners, that through shipwreck are cast out of any vessel, or perish by less thereof, and land themselves on our shore. Their peril, loss of ship, and spoil of goods being wreck enough, for which instead of robbing them of what the devouring sea has left them, we not only commiserate them, but with the faithful restoration of their own, repair all their otherwise irrecoverable losses, if any survive to declare them. If none can claim them, then the next treasury must have them. This injurious custom of adding affliction to affliction is I confess too frequent with you Europeans that live upon the seacoasts, and gape for such booties, calling such wreck God's-good, which you unjustly detain as your own in the devil's name. But on the contrary, to prevent such calamities, we set up constantly, nights, several Pharos or lights on high hills and towers to direct the seafaring passengers how to avoid both rocks and pirates. And for their better security by way of prevention, we suffer no ship to go forth without six very skillful pilots in it at least, and those well approved of by the admiralty.

"We have for the better advance of naviga- tion and increase of expert pilots a constant lecture of it in the three principle maritime cities, the readers of which science are to instruct our mariners in all maritime causes, in penning and reducing sea-fight into an art, as

many have done land service, and as your Sir
Walter Raleigh attempted the same (whose directions therein it were to be wished were to be
found out and augmented), in the principles of
Astronomy, Geometry, and the art of swimming and
diving, so necessary to recover goods lost and
sunk in the bottom of the sea; and these have a
large allowance from our admiral, to prevent
those often shipwrecks which through the rawness
and inexperience of the seamen might otherwise
happen.

"We have in our hot baths, for the true
rectifying and cleansing of diseased bodies, able
physicians allowed of by the college, at a certain stipend to examine the state of every body
that shall go into, or take into them any purging
or cleansing waters; none being permitted to use
them without their approbation. This is to prevent the death of many by the errors of a few
unskilled empirics, who not rightly understanding
the true economy and state of their patients'
bodies, or finding out the peccant* humors and
parts worst affected, commonly expel humors less
offensive to their final prejudice. The like care
is taken in all cities and towns that no apothe-
caries, surgeons, women, or empirics shall admin-
ister physic to any patient or prepare it, not so
much as to their own husbands, wives, children or

* Morbid

servants, without the physicians special advice and direction appointed for that place.

"We have great encouragements for all ingenious persons, and give great honor and reverence as well as large rewards to the authors of all new and good treatises, whether divine or humane, of all artificial inventions, discoverers of new countries, minerals, earths, waters, or whatsoever else is useful to mankind; either at home by rewarding them with great pensions, or from abroad by erecting their statues.

"We study the public good so much that whereas we reward those that discover, so he is in some measure punished that conceals and hides a benefit which may pleasure his country, for they that do no good when they can, as well as they that do mischief, are here accounted debtors alike and are looked on as unnatural children to their common parent, their country."

This said, he offered me the view of their codes and presidents, if at any time I pleased to come to the seminary of law students to be farther instructed in their laws and form of government. Here, I rising up, made a low obeisance and kissed the hem of his tippet again, giving him many and large thanks for the favor he had already done in imparting to me so many wholesome laws and divine constitutions. And though he seemed willing to enlarge the converence at that time, wishing me to sit down again by him; yet to prevent me of that happiness in came immediately a messenger with a red tip-staff gilt at both ends, in his hand, and whispered him away about some urgent affairs. Whereupon, troubled a little to leave me so abruptly, he turned to me and said, "My friend, at this time I must ask your pardon, being commanded hence in haste; tomorrow or any day next week if you please to see our seminary I shall be at more leisure, and glad to enlarge myself farther to you." So he left me, and as he went out caused the delinquent to be taken forth the pillory; whence descending he fell down upon his bare knees and asked the alcaldorem and all Christian people whom he had by his ill example offended, forgiveness. This done, and the judge forgiving him, and giving him a short monitory charge, he went about his affairs, whilst the poor offender was led away to receive the other part of his punishment.

The next day my intended visit to the alcaldorem was prevented, for Joabin came that morning early to see me and told us "(Sirs) you are like to be enriched three days hence at the next city about two Karans and a half of with the regalie of as pleasing an entertainment, and specious show, as I believe your eyes have ever beheld. For the ingenious Verdugo (so was he called) that has of late found out the way of making linen cloth, and consequently paper of asbestos or living linen, that fire shall not consume the writing (which paper is called salamandrian) by the help of some mineral powders and the spirit of vitriol, is, being born and bred there, for this his rare invention now there to be honored by the chief of all the city and province and after feast and other ceremonies and pastimes to receive his reward. This according to the custom is always made proportionable to the worth of the invention and the merits of the person. "I shall therefore," said he, "provide a convenient place for you and your fellows where you shall all see his graceful entry into the city, and entertainment afterwards at the great hall of Solomon's House where I will also provide for you a standing to behold the triumphs, to hear the speech which is to be expressed in the Spanish tongue, as also a pastoral interlude." We all thanked him for this his noble offer, being exceeding joyful at the news. The prefixed day being come, conducted by him we all got thither betimes* on mules he provided, and took our stands near the Gate St. Mark (the gates there taking their names from the churches they stand next to) where all the nobles, magistrates and chief citizens splendidly equipped met Verdugo on horseback, and welcomed him at his first entry.

He was a middle-sized man, of sprightly mien and ingenuous countenance, discovering in his bold aspect a subtle vivacity and promptness to

* Seasonably, in good time.

76

undertake and perform great things. Here appeared forty proper men on horseback, all clad in crimson satin loose coats. Immediately after them and before Verdugo's chariot, a stately pageant no less glorious than the other was drawn with four black horses abreast, richly trapped and plumed, wherein on an imperial throne, a fair youth, personating Minerva the Goddess of Invention was seated, holding forth in her right hand a roll of paper, fired at both ends, as who would say, lighting Verdugo to his crown of glory. This emblem (as he told me) is ever varied according to the present invention. Verdugo followed mounted on a high triumphal chariot of gilt cedar, drawn by four milk-white jennets abreast, and those trapped with scarlet and silver-embroidered velvet. His vestment was like himself, youthful both for fashion, garb, and color, being of a grass-green satin, made close to the body, and over it a mantle of the same richly embroidered, and lined with cloth of silver, carelessly hanging over one shoulder. On his head he wore a light gold laurel enameled with green, through which his auburn locks, both long and curling, burnished and shone like so many sunbeams. By his side he wore a silver hilted sword, tied in a fair crimson taffeta embroidered scarf, which weapon (as Joabin told me) was only permitted to these triumphant inventors to wear ever after in the city to maintain and vindicate themselves the sole authors of that their invention against all counterfeit pretenders or gain-saying opposers.

To this end he wore a bright gauntlet also on his
right hand instead of his glove; the other being
carried by one on horseback immediately before
him. Close behind his chariot attended the nobles, magistrates, gentry, and citizens, two and
two; the chief on horseback, the rest on foot;
the streets and windows (which were richly carpeted) being thronged with orderly and silent
spectators. Whilst they all advanced thus towards
the great hall, this first part of the show being
past, the Jew hastily conducted us a back way to
the palace, that we might there be seated before
the rest came, to prevent the press of people
that flocked thither as it were to some coronation. As soon as Verdugo came into the great
court before the hall (which echoed with trumpets
and other loud instruments) they all lighted from
their horses attending Verdugo on foot, who then
alighted also from his chariot; and at his entrance into the hall was embraced with both arms
(by that same Father that before had given me his
blessing) and who there stood with the Fraternity
of the House ready to receive him. Close by him
one of the chief and most eloquent brethren delivered there a most elegant speech. The effect
of it was the commendation of learning in general, with a particular account of that his late
invention, extolling the admirable ingenuity
thereof for the perpetual advance of learning,
with a full exemplification of the good and benefit that did indubitably accrue not to themselves
only but to all posterity, and concluding with

great thanks to the happy inventor of that noble art, and praises to God the enlightener of our understandings, and sole Author and giver of all good things. This gratulatory Eulogium being finished, the Father of Solomon's House took off his green upper mantle, and invested him with Minerva's long robe which was a stole down to the ground, silk and silver flowers in needlework. Minerva then took off his former laurel, and placed her own garland upon his head which was most elegant for composure, adorned with all the variety of the choicest flowers expressed in their proper native colors, and to the life shadowed forth in silk, gold, and silver. Over it was super-added a crown of divers rays, in each of which in fine engravery the names of all the most ingenious authors and inventors since our first Altabin's time (who was the first king of this island) were curiously inserted. This done, the Father laying his right hand bare upon his head blessed him (as he was presented to him on his knees by Minerva) saying: "God bless you, my son, and enlighten your great understanding more and more, for the benefit of mankind and this our Island of Bensalem. We admit you now as fellow, brother and companion into this our Society." Here Verdugo, having bowed and kissed the verge of his tippet, the Father lifted him up with his right hand and fixed him on his legs again, and immediately presented him with a great silver basin full charged with 5,000 ducats of gold, declaring farther that besides that gratuity from the Society, the State was pleased to reward his great deserts with the yearly pension of 5,000 ducats more to him and his posterity. Thereupon he requested him to declare his invention with the true manner of effecting it according to custom for the public good of the state and benefit of mankind. The reason of this their custom (as Joabin told me) was not so much to prevent monopolizing or engrossing that beneficial commodity to himself whereby he only might bend his bad wares (which would be but the enriching of one man to beggar many) but chiefly to instruct others also in it, that the invention should not perish with the author; and be rather meliorated and augmented by the emulous wits of ingenious imitators. Then after he had presented to him in writing the schedule of the true manner of perfecting that work, the Father took him by the left hand and Minerva by the right, leading him thus between them into the next great room (which was richly hung and carpeted, and where he was sumptiously feasted; all the house in the interim echoing with variety of sweet music, sometimes still, otherwise loud, sometimes resounding with joyful acclamations, and sometimes again with soft melodious songs, the first proclaiming, the last whispering the praises, worth, and merits of the ever-famed Verdugo.

While they were feasting within, Joabin told me that so soon as dinner was ended, the Father was to record the invention in a book of that salamandrian paper Verdugo had presented them, with his the author's name and surname, and place of birth and the true manner of effecting it, the inventor himself being by, to attest it his invention under his own hand. "This book of register," said he, "is carefully there to be prevented in Solomon's House to all perpetuity."

Then leading me into a long and large gallery by the hall, he showed me the statues of all the prime inventors in many ages before, wherewith that spacious room was above almost furnished round. Amongst the rest he first pointed out the inventor of paper, whose name (as he there showed it me underwritten) was Papyrius, whence it took its first denomination; and not from the Egyptian papyri or sedgy weeds they first used ("as you Europeans," said he, "...conjecturally suppose) being pressed into thin flakes or leaves and dried, to write on. "For this same Papyrius," he added, "first invented our paper made with rags in King Ptolomey's time, a little before he raised his famous library at Alexandria. Then he showed me the effigies in transparent crystal of the unfortunate inventor of vitrum ductile or malleable glass, whose invention Tiberius rewarded with death, and just underneath it this epitaph written:

He who gave life to glass and to himself, like a bee enclosed in amber and more translucent than his own, renders hard this

monument more durable* than bronze, an artificer. While Tiberius killed him, the glass-
maker, he could not thaw away his invention.

Next to that was the portrait of him that
first invented the <u>pixis</u> <u>nautica</u>, or sea chart to
sail by; and this <u>account</u> of the person under it:

He who hit upon the needle and pointed out
the use of the needle, sprung from the land
di Lavoro, and teaching to swim, himself
stands in the skies as the bear, Flavius.

Then he pointed to me the ingenious inventor
of preserving gunpowder from taking fire, by
which preservative art, learned probably from
hence, the <u>Venetian</u> <u>arsenals,</u> <u>magazines</u>, and
cities are preserved from ruin, under which to
the eternal memory of the author I read these
four lines:

If Prometheus stole the fire from heaven,
this other man (stole) lightening+ from na-
tron dust, Gasparus Botallus: O divine
thefts, which in the meantime bid us be safe!

Close by him was the portrait of <u>Magellanus</u>,
his ship called the Victory, sailing, and of

* A line from Homer.
+ Sulphur

82

himself on the upper deck of it; and underneath
it these verses inscribed:

I was the first to circle the globe on my
course with flying sails, Magellan, steered
by you as my guide in an unknown sea. I
sailed around and justly am called Victoria;
now my sails are my wings, my prize in my
glory, my battle the sea.

And next by him he showed me with a certain
asterism of high remark, the bold Sir Francis
Drake, pictured also sailing on a little globe,
who next after Magellanus, he told me, girdled
the world, with these verses underwritten:

Drake, whom the end of the world he roamed
through has come to know, whom each pole of
the world saw once; if men should be silent,
the stars would make you known, (for) the sun
does not know how to forget its own companion.

Almost next to this he showed me the ingenious fantasy of the painter Palaton, who had
portrayed Homer, that Prince of Poets, vomiting,
and all the rest of them licking it up, with this
distich* written underneath it:

Look at the Maeonide, by whom the mouths of

* An epigram of two verses.

83

the poets are bedewed by Pierian waters, as
if from a perennial fount.

Close to this stood that elaborate and most
incentive piece of Venus, which Praxiteles drew
so to the life that a young man fell in love with
it, with this distich under it:

Ixion falls desperately in love with a cloud,
a young man with this shadow, yet this is not
the shade of a goddess, but Venus herself.

By it was Myron's brazen heifer, so lively
expressed it deceived both the herd and pastor,
as it almost did myself (said he) at my first
beholding it; with this epigram affixed:

I am the heifer of my creator Myron, made in
heaven of bronze; not made, I believe, but
born: (for) thus the bull enters me, thus the
next heifer lows, thus the thirsty calf seeks
our udders, are you amazed that I feel the
herd? The master of the herd himself is wont
to count me among the grazing beasts.

Near these he pointed out the famous statues
and pictures of those Italian painters Michael
Angelo and Raphael Urbin, whose physiognomies
were drawn to the life severally with their own
hands; and by them that of Durerus of Noringberg,
under whose these lines as his epitaph were written:

Here that famous painter of Germany, already tired, draws his inimitable hand away from a painting. Apelles, were he now alive, would grant to him the glory of the palm of victory.

On the other side omitting many of lesser note, he showed me the statue of Simon Stevinius, that excellent inventor of geometrical engines and proportions, and of the sailing coaches, sitting himself in a coach of black marble that seemed to travail without horses; and underneath it these verses written:

Typhis* drew a ship swift as wind into the seas, Jupiter brought his house to the stars of the sky; Stevinius' excellence brought him to a terrestrial place: for your work had not been Typhis' nor that work Jupiter's.

Next under him, as well worthy so to be placed, stood the head only of the ingenious Boniger erect upon a brazen winged column. This is the man (said he) who first gave the vigorous motion to the ship, that by the help of an artificial prime mover within it, and but one man to move the same engine (which is placed on the side of the vessel) it sails without help of oars, in the greatest calm, and sometimes against wind and tide. "This is the man that contrived the horizontal sails, by which three ploughs may go

*Greek typhos = whirlwind

85

together, and at one time both plough, sow and harrow. The same man likewise," said he, "invented the flying chariots to be born up in the air," underneath whose effigies these words in great gilt letters were written:

The lord of winds and ocean here rides, ship-wrecked in the shoals.
                                    Thomas Boniger.

Next to him he showed me the statue of J. Neper, Baron of Merchiston, who first invented the whole use of logarithms. And next to him were erected the statues of Johannes Regiomontanus, who made the wooden eagle and iron fly; and Erasmus Rheinhold, who transcended all in the rules of tangents and secants. And not far from these he signally pointed out the statue of that most learned geometrian Thomas Harriot, who was the first, he told me, that found out the quadrature of the circle, etc. "There is also," said he, "...the perfect effigy of your learned Dr. Harvey, the happy author of the blood's circulation," which I viewed with this inscription underneath it:

He who gave movement of circulation to the blood is here, a perpetual stayer.
                                    Dr. John Harveyus.

"With the prospect of more of these your European inventors, as the inventors of clocks

and pendulums, of wind-guns and wind-jacks, of
stenography, and chorography, the ingenious con-
triver of preserving the chimneys from smoking;
of the Reviellirs, which at the same instant
sound the alarm, strike fire, light the candle,
and of making the tenth part of fire serve for
brewing by placing the cauldron and making the
furnace exactly; of the expulsative powder; of
making a little vessel to swim under water undiscovered, to blow up ships, bridges and houses;
with many other of our own island inventors (all
whose excellent pictures are either in tables, or
engraved, or cast in brass or other metals), I
could entertain you longer, but since you are now
here I will otherwise entertain your fancy (least
too much of the same should breed a nausea) in
showing you those rarities of nature and philosophical secrets which being not vulgar will by
the vulgar scarce be understood or believed."

Thereupon he carried me to a little closet
at the end of that gallery, whose door at his
first knock one of the fraternity opened, who
with complacent desire to satisfy my greedy curi-
osity was willing to expose whatsoever rarity
Joabin pleased to call for. Joabin told him that
for his part he dare not be so bold, but whatsoever he please freely to communicate or let us
see, he should take for a very great favor.
Hereupon he immediately reached forth of a little
ark wherein many rarities were placed, [includ-
ing] a loadstone far bigger than that which holds

up <u>Mahomet's</u> tomb in <u>Mecca</u>. "This is the truly precious stone of such divine use," said he, "...that by its charitable direction it not only cements the divided world into one body politic, maintaining trade and society with the remotest parts and nations, but is in many other things of rare use and service. I shall not open all its properties (said he), most of them being already known amongst you <u>Europeans</u>. I will only unfold this useful and most admirable conclusion upon it, and which has been but lately here experimentally discovered, which is this. Two needles of equal size being touched together at the same time with this stone, and severally set on two tables with the alphabet written circularly about them; two friends, thus prepared and agreeing on the time, may correspond at never so great a distance. For by turning the needle in one alphabet, the other in the distant table will by a secret sympathy turn itself after the like manner. This secret was first experimented here by one <u>Lamoran</u>, who being suspected of apostacy because of his great intimacy with one <u>Alchmerin</u>, his friend and a Jew, and his little adhesion to some of his opinions, was sent into the island of <u>Conversion</u> close prisoner; who there to hold constant intelligence with his intimate, first found out this admirable invention." And therewith he showed me those two very tables by which, during that his confinement, thus they communicated their thoughts each to other. He next showed me a <u>Selenoscope</u> to view the moon, stars

and new planets, and a rare microscope wherein
the eyes, legs, mouth, hair and eggs of a cheese-
mite, as well as the blood running in the veins
of a louse, was easily to be discerned.

Then he brought forth the great burning-
glass which Proclus made, wherein the sunbeams
contracted might like lightning fire ships at a
very great distance. The same, he told me, Archimedes imitated when the Romans beseiged Syracuse.
Here is also, said he, that ductile glass, which
Faber the inventor thereof first presented to
Tiberius Caesar, which is so pliable that it is
not easily to be broken, yielding to the stroke
of the hammer like silver or iron, and which
though we daily make of the same, we preserve as
a sacred relic in memory of the inventor whom he
put to death. Then he produced out of a large
vial some of that powder [which] is called sympa-
thetical, and is now grown common in Europe also.
"This is," said he, "...the most salubrious balsam in the world, and cures all wounds that are
not mortal, in a very short time, at distance. It
is made only of the purest vitriol calcined white
in the sun, to which we add the gum of traga-
canth; this strewed on the bloody cloth or weapon, the spirits of the vitriol incorporating
with the blood, the wound by attraction of light
and of the sun heals; the atoms and spirits of
the blood by diffusion participating either heat
or cold. So that if the wound be kept clean only,
and in moderate heat (as this incorporation of

blood and powder on the cloth must be), in three
days the wound shall be cicatrized and perfectly
healed. And without it I wonder why you Europeans
will go where wars and fightings are so much in
request and so frequent."

Then out of a little box he produced some of
that powder which he called expulsative, ten
grains of which mixed (said he) with half the
ordinary quantity of gunpowder for a charge shall
send the bullet as far again out of a cannon, as
a full charge of the other simply, and do the
same execution; and so proportionably to the
powder out of lesser guns.

"These two lamps which you here behold,"
said he, "...shining in these two large and
close-stopped vials are of incumbustible oil
which (so as no air comes to it) will never be
extinct, the oil being composed of a bituminous
liquor and that pitchy naptha which flows out of
a kind of brimstone-lime near Babylon."

Then he showed me (for to me as a stranger
he most addressed himself) Archimedes' silver
sphere of heaven where the sun, moon, and planets
kept their orderly courses according to nature as
the fixed stars their set stations by an artificial engine within moving each wheel and sphere
to true and exact distance of time and proportion
of figure. The like, said he, your Emperor
Ferdinand sent to Suleiman, the great Turk, but

that was nothing so exact or near so large as this.

Then he brought a small vial of rarified water in which the dust of a rose or any other plant incinerated and burned to ashes, the remaining salt surviving in those ashes and put into that revivifying liquor, the rose or plant shall resume its pristine shape and color.

Then he showed me ordinary ice, petrified and so hardened by art (he said) that it was as useful as ordinary glass or crystal, though not so transparent, and which no small fire should thaw. With several other the like rarities he entertained me till such time as the feast was ended, and Verdugo's invention was enrolled. And then, with thanks given to him for this great favor, Joabin led me back to the rest of our fellows who kept their stations in the great hall, whither we saw Verdugo led and attended back in the same order he went thence, and seated in a chair of crimson velvet at the foot of a little throne covered with the same and richly embroidered with gold, having a rich canopy of state over it of the same in the midst of the stage whereon sat the Father of Solomon's House that had adopted him. On the other side at his foot on a cushion of state somewhat lower sat Minerva. Hereon after most ravishing music and several scenes silently represented to the eye was acted to life with Roscian mien a pleasant and most facetious comedy in which the arts were all in witty contentions emulous of precedency. The pastoral being ended, and all the other scenes in curious landscape represented to the admiration and joy of each spectator, the Father descended from his throne, and gave Verdugo thanks in the name of Solomona and behalf of the whole island for his great industry, care and pains in the happy discovery and effecting of that his noble invention, wishing God might bless and prosper all his future endeavors. Verdugo returned his thanks also with a grateful acknowledgement after mutual embraces and solemn leave-taking, and then all the company as silent as the night (which was then almost approached) dissolved, each one betaking himself to his several home, and we to ours upon our mules, which there at the gate stood ready for us. The next morning I went betime to the seminary of law students which was a fair and spacious building consisting of three large courts, in the middlemost whereof the Alcaldorems inhabit, the other two being filled with the Procuratorans, Advocatorems, and other officers of smaller note belonging to that society. In the midsts of this middle court on the right hand of it (as I was directed) I ascended about six steps, and then entered the lodgings of that good and learned Alcaldorem (who before had invited me thither) those being very spatious, neat and gravely furnished. He was not married (as few of the Alcaldorems there be) not that they are inhibited marriage but in case they

be not martyred before they are advanced to the
seat of judicature, they seldom marry after.
Partly to avoid the jealousy of others through
the temptation of a covetous wife who may be
wrought upon with gifts to move the judge in
private to favor such or such a party, or at
least be suspected so to do, and partly to avoid
the trouble of economics, their whole time being
taken up in the study of the laws and the due
administration of public justice. For they are
very intent and upright (as the Jew had informed
me) never listening to any cause before it be
brought before then in open court, to be decided
immediately upon hearing. After he had led me
through a long gallery furnished round with the
most eminent alcaldorem's pictures of that island, he brought me into a very fair library
consisting altogether of lawbooks, civil, canon,
and municipal of all nations, at the upper end of
which in golden characters on black marble was
God's Law inscribed, which he delivered to Moses
in the Ten Commandments. Now, my friend, said he,
not to let you wander in this labyrinth of learning, I shall show you according to my promise the
Codes and Institutes of Law particularly belonging to this our island of Bensalem." At which I
bowed and followed him close as he conducted me
by the hand to the upper end of that library
where opening the door of a fair inner repository
just underneath the Law of Moses he brought me
into that lesser Vatican whence out of a gilded
ark all covered with mosaic work of the best

sort, he took me out a fair folio rarely bound
and covered with crimson velvet and embossed with
gold. Herein, he told me, this being one of the
ten Codes, was the fundamental law not of that
island alone but of all other kingdoms and nations, this being the original whence all other
national constitutes were first derived. Having
unclasped it and opened its leaves full of red
characters, he offered it me to kiss first, which
I did, and then to peruse. But though the hands
were all seemingly very legible, yet being written by their several kings in their native language, which I so little understood, I humbly
requested him that as he had already been pleased
to dilate upon them so that he would also do me
the favor farther to interpret. Herein he showed
a great willingness to inform me farther, but to
prevent me of that happiness an Alguazillan summoned him away to do speedy justice. This must
not at all be neglected; therefore he said: "My
friend, have me excused at this time; when I am
at leisure you shall command me farther." So he
went immediately and put on his purple robe while
I took my humble leave of him and went home.

The next day Joabin came to us and would
needs show us the city, which had but superfi-
cially viewed before, with the several churches,
palaces, noblemen's houses, hospitals, nosoco-
mies*, gardens, groves, grottoes, and other
    * Related to hospital; (from the Greek nosos:
sickness, & komein: to care for).

rarities of greatest fame in it. This was, as he told me, the largest, most beautiful and populous city, next to the imperial one wherein Solomona resides, of the whole island. This Bellatore (so was the city we lived in called) was situated upon a little rise in an open level country, and about some eight miles in circuit. Two sides of it were environed with a large watergraft, and within upon the verge or bank set with six rows in equal distance with tall pine and fir trees. It had twelve gates and twenty-four towers, two towers being placed between every gate of equal height and bigness. The whole fabric of buildings, which was all of one height in the same street, was seated within the walls without any adjoining suburbs. The streets (which were all thirty foot in breadth) were paved through with great stones of marble, such as the houses were all built with on the sides, and in the midst with large round and very smooth stones, the drills and water channels being on each side of the highway near the houses. Every house there had leaden cisterns to preserve all the rainwater that fell from the houses, this being for the many uses conceived better than any other. But the most necessary use of it is, at any drought when the springs should chance to fail or the pipes be faulty. At each door of their houses also they had lesser receptacles for the urine which they used for some lands, as well as to make saltpeter with. On each side of the streets were marble pillared cloisters to walk dry under

in the winter and cool in the summer, some of the
pillars being inlaid with jasper, onyx, and other
precious stones. Almost through the midst of the
city ran the stately river Guavalare, famous for
his spring in curing many diseases. Upon this
river within the walls stood six stately strong
bridges, so broad and so high that ships of good
burden might sail under them. The citadel was
environed as in an island with this stately river
and fortified with two wet grafts besides, to
which there were no passages but by drawbridges
and those countersituated. Having shown me that
also with its inexpugnable strength (which is
rarely permitted to any strangers especially), he
led me to the Christ Church Cathedral, situated
upon the highest part in the city, next that
whereon the citadel stands, which overlooked and
commanded all the town. From a pleasant tower of
this Mother Church he showed me at once the
resplendent glory of the whole town, the curious
pile whereof being compact of such uniform buildings all covered with copper, beautified with
gilt pinnacles and high, well-formed towers, was
so pleasant a prospect that I stood amazed and
dazzled with the luster, being unwilling to move
thence, I was so ravished with admiration and
delight. We descended at last into the body of
the church, in which were no pews for any to sit
and sleep in, only several rows of mats thick set
for the people to kneel on; for ease, he told
me, "...helps devotion, whereas hardship and
suffering at it distracts the mind and makes it

seem tedious." Here the women kneel or stand
about the upper part of it surrounded with the
females of their families that they may not be
seen of the men who stand lower amidst their male
servants. The first custom is to teach their
families good discipline by example abroad, the
latter of parting the sexes is to prevent dis-
traction, and that adultery which may be committed with the eye. To this purpose the men there
wore black cypress veils, though they were bare-
headed, and the women white veils over their
heads and face, loosely hanging. It was odorifer-
ous, lightsome, and glorious; the heavenly music
always resounding between both the sacrifices of
morning and evening without any noise or discourse. The gates always in the daytime stood
open, the men entering and going out always at
once, and the women at another. Here he showed me
the most elegant picture of the Church Militant,
mysteriously but lively drawn by <u>Titian</u> in a
large table, and hung on the southside wall. The
arms under it were thus displayed: over a field
argent watered with tears <u>gutte gules</u>*, a chief
<u>nebulae sable</u>+. Underneath them was this motto in

* Gutte: in heraldry, sprinkled with drops.
Gules: in heraldry, red, as a tincture; represented in engraved escutcheons by vertical lines
closely set.
+ Neubulae sable: in heraldry, made up of short,
black curves. Chief: in heraldry, upper part of
the escutcheon.

their own language, which he rendered to me in Spanish: <u>Tears</u> <u>and</u> <u>prayers</u> <u>are</u> <u>the</u> <u>church's</u> <u>Arms</u>. On the one side of it was the picture at large of <u>Hierusalem</u> and the <u>Savior</u> weeping over it. On the other the portrait of him in his zeal scourging the buyers and sellers out of the Temple, most expressively drawn to the life by the same hand, with this holy text underneath it in Greek, <u>My</u> <u>house</u> <u>shall</u> <u>be</u> <u>called</u> <u>a</u> <u>house</u> <u>of</u> <u>prayer</u>. Right opposite on the north side wall stood that large and famous original of <u>Michael</u> <u>Angelo</u> which depicted our <u>Savior's</u> second coming at the day of Judgment. In short, it was everywhere adorned with the choicest and most divine pieces that were ever anywhere to be seen.

Having viewed the church round with all its decent bravery, curious sculptures, and rare antiquities, with its library (which each church, he told me, there had one) he returned home with me, and by the way informed me of a splendid appearance <u>Solomona</u> was to make in public the third day after upon occasion of a great horse-race with other innocent pastimes wherewith the people entertained the king that whole day. "Now if yourself," said he, "...or as many as will of your company, please to go to the imperial city, you shall ride thitherward tomorrow morning, and there I shall use the means that you shall not only kiss our <u>Solomona's</u> stole, but behold the gaieties and solemnities of that grand appearance, with the modest port and quiet government of that glorious court, and the magnificent structures thereof.

Hereat having anticipated these future prospects by a right supposal of their transcendent excellencies beyond all we had yet seen, I accepted of his kind offer with great joy and alacrity, and told him that since he was pleased to undertake the trouble we would all attend him that voyage at the day. Joabin then taking his leave at the door of the Stranger's House, whither his civility had returned me, willed me and the rest of our company that designed that voyage (which he hoped would be all) to be ready in our best equipage very early next morning when he would not fail to be with us. The wished for morning no sooner appeared but Joabin accompanied with thirteen carioles desired that the whole company would be spectators of that solemn festivity to which purpose he had brought (he said) carioles enough and those convenient for us all. His importunity would not admit of any denial, so that we all ascended into them as he had ordered our places, and advanced somewhat before sunrise. Sometimes drawn by land and otherwise at certain stages by water, that evening we arrived at a convenient vento or inn in the midway where we had all conveniences and respect imaginable besides our entertainment which was gratis to us strangers only. The next morning we again prevented the sun by our early advance, in regard we were to reach the court that day, which we did in

good time with much ease and pleasure. But by the
way, a little before noon, we entered one of the
three universities wherein was the most famous
college of agriculture that the island afforded.
Here after we had refreshed ourselves, to pass
away two or three hours of the hottest part of
the day, he brought me acquainted with the Providoran General, and Principal then of that famous
college. A reverend old man he was, and no less
learned in the history of nature, then full of
courteous humanity both in his discourse and
carriage. He first led us into a very fair physic
garden, wherein he told us were almost as many
medicinal plants and herbs as he believed Solomon
knew, at least as are anywhere now to be found
serviceable for the use of man or beast. Having
observed there the many rarities, he was pleased
to show me particularly there growing, as the
sensible plant, semper-vivum, saffron, licorice,
rice, caraway, anise, gromwell, virga aurea,
elicampane, with many more. He took me by the
hand and led me a little out of the town over the
river on the backside of that garden which environed that other great nursery (as he called it)
and contained about a thousand acres. "Herein,"
said he, "...we daily try several experiments of
setting, sowing, planting, grafting, inoculating,
ameliorating the earth with several composts: as
the dry with marl; the lean and hungry with dung
of pigeons, men, or horses, soot, sea sand or
ooze, chalk, etc.; the sandy with mud; the cold
with ashes; the rich with brakes, straw,

seaweeds, folding of sheep, etc., all which, as
we find the ground, we use and apply to it. But
if you delight in husbandry, which is but the
quickening of Nature by art, I shall briefly tell
you of some of our customs of remark," which discourse I greedily embracing, whilst we sat together in a cool shady grotto by the riverside,
he farther hinted to me thus: that in that pilot
which belonged to his college of agriculture, of
which he was (he said) the Principal, they dug
all the ground, because the spade goes deeper
than the plough, and kills all weeds and grass
best. "All our study here is to improve a little
ground well with little pains and charges. For we
conceive the well improving of a small island
better than the conquering of a new large kingdom. That we may do this in all places alike and
to the purpose, we use the means, and they are
these: we buy in all commons, for they rather
make poor than maintain them; therefore those
which we have had were either long since bought
in by the Providorans in every particular province or divided by them amongst the inhabitants
adjoining who had right therein, according to
their right and due proportions; one such acre
thus enclosed and improved being now more beneficial to the meanest of them than four were before
in common. Next we search all grounds for iron,
tin, lead, gold, silver, and all other beneficial
things whatsoever; likewise we enjoin all husbandmen to search their grounds for beneficial
earths such as marl, chalk, fuller's earth and

the like, in the search of which they often find several precious stones, useful composts, and medicinal earths.

"Though we breed many stout horses towards the maritime parts, that by looking on the sea they may acquire more fierceness and become more emboldened for field-service; they being here seldom employed otherwise. Yet we conceive that oxen being less subject to diseases and maintained with less cost and trouble, and will suffer more hardship, toil and labor are fitter than horses for the plough or wagon, and are here therefore most used. In many places also, especially where the streets are even, we use great mastiff dogs (of which here we breed many) to draw up and down the streets things upon sledges, made low on purpose and running on four little wheels. By this means one stout dog that is fed with little or no charge shall carry or draw as much as any three men. That we may not want workmen, the Providoran furnishes us on the sudden with harvestmen, either of the condemned collar-men or other freemen out of the adjoining next city. So that in one day, notice beforehand given him, any man's harvest may be cut and inned with little charge and trouble. That these country farmers may live plentifully, pay their rent and lay up, every farm of such a value is to maintain so many hives of bees for wax and honey, with which as with currants, raspberries, damsons, mulberries, cherries, pinapples, pears, and

apples (of which last we have above 200 species),
many excellent drinks are made to keep their
families and sell besides. And that they may not
want good wines, besides what the vineyards af-
ford, each one on the southside of all his
houses, stables, barns, and outhouses is bound to
set the best grapes that thus they may soonest
ripen. For firing and other necessary uses, they
are enjoined to plant in all their woods (especially near home) swift growers, as the abletree,
the ash, sallow aspen, willow, for hoops and
hopples. Likewise they are enjoined to plant near
their houses almonds, olives, chestnuts, walnuts,
and quinces. Those whose farms are of the largest
value are obliged to maintain so many boxes of
silkworms, for the keeping of which they are to
plant mulberry trees proportionable, on whose
leaves they feed with little charge. The great
product and gain by them (as he demonstrated,
together with the ways of preserving them, which
were very ingenious) is, said he, scarce credi-
ble. Our next chief care is to prevent mischiefs,
and in paticular mildews and smuttiness of corn;
1. by changing each year the species of grain; 2.
by limiting the ground and corn, which last pre-
serves it from birds and worms also. For preserving your orchard, we first prune the trees well
from moss, mistletoe, and suckers, sometimes
opening the roots and relieving them with a new
compost. In short those things which grow best of
slips, as currants, quinces, codlings, gooseber-
ries, etc., we never set the kernals, though

others are best to set, which we do accordingly as experience teaches for the best."

We likewise enjoin those farmers of the best value of all to maintain fishponds and decoys, that thus when the weather is not seasonable to shoot flying, they may be sure of fowl at all times. To prevent his farther discourse in came two gardeners with each of them a large cornucop-ia in his hand, full of all the variety of fruit the season then afforded. Having tasted some of the choicest he recommended, with some of his choicer cool drinks and wines of the place, he made us taste afresh of his singular humanity by accompanying us back to our inn, where he civilly left us, and where the rest of our company (though the envious time would not) tarried for and waited on us.

Arrived at last at the full view of the palace, we stood enamored with the delicious prospect of that vast emporium, it being the largest city of that kingdom, though altogether unfortified, except with faithful citizens, for thus open lay all the inland cities. There were we carried to the Stranger's House, another stately place built according to the model of the former but somewhat larger, where our quiet repose and splendid entertainment made us forget our former travels.

Now the morning star no sooner appeared to usher in the third day's light, but <u>Joabin</u> came again to us to conduct us to the <u>Grand Palace</u>, where having led us through many fair streets and stately <u>piazzas</u>, we at last came to the <u>imperial palace</u> whose magnificent and mighty structure at first view made us stand amazed. Before it was a spacious court, thickset with tall cypress trees, pines and jasmines in rows, in the midst of which a white marble fountain was erected and held up by eight brazen lions, each of them according to the antique Roman manner pouring out of their mouths the crystalline water. Over the portal of the <u>palace</u>, whose bases and chapters were of polished marble and gilded imagery, were <u>Justice</u> and <u>Fortitude</u> in their proper habit described; the gates themselves being all of gilt cedar, very high and stately.

The <u>palace</u> was quadrant, and at each corner a high tower (which seemed to be of shining <u>jasper</u>, for here they but adorn their houses and walls with them, having no other opinion of precious stones than of painted glass or shells, which for their diversity of colors please the eye only, having in themselves no real intrinsic value) erected its stately head. All the walls both within and without were splendidly decked with the statues of all the Roman <u>emperors, virgins</u>, and <u>matrons</u>, and with divers other famous antiquities; the windows (whose bars were of silver) being all very high, double-leafed and of

square malleable glass. In the first court, which
was 180 yards square and called Martial, the
pillars and arches were all of mosaic work and
supported with lions, tigers, lynxes, leopards,
and griffins, so lively cast in brass and painted
that they looked as if they would assail the
spectators that approached them. In the midst of
this court an obelisk of wonderful art, all of
shining copper, set forth on the one side the
proud squadrons of the Romans and on the other
the Carthaginian camp in warlike equipage; the
valiant Hannibal leading the one army, and that
invincible African Scipio the other. On the other
side stood those masculine spirits, Fabius Maxi-
mus the buckler of Rome, and Marcus Furius Camil-
lus the sword, fighting in the high capitol in
his country's defense; Mutius Scaevola, Caesar,
Pompey, Alexander, and Marcus Varro the happy
consul. Of the Spanish heroes, Theodosius the
Great, the valiant Cid Ruis, Dias, Bernard del
Carpio, Hernand, Goncales, Fonseca, Don Lewis of
Villanova, Sancho, Ferdinanado, and Charles the
Emperor. Of the French chieftains, none but Charles the Great, the founder of the Western empire,
and the late puissant Henry the Fourth. Right
opposite stood all the valiant opposers of the
Muhammadan Empire, particularly those of the
Venetian state, and Matthias Corvinus. A little
above all stood the invincible Johannes Hunnea-
des, his father, armed all over from head to
foot, brandishing a naked sword in his right
hand, with many dead men's skulls, heads, and

arms at his feet. This is that renowned Hungarian, said Joabin, who so valiantly resisted the Turks incursions, and slew of them 50,000 at the battle of Naxon. After we had sufficiently beheld these heroic champions, he led us up into a large rich hall, whose ceiling was of carved ivory, and walls embellished with most lively portraits. There was Lucretia killing herself in very earnest, and Artemis wailing over her husband Mausolus's monument, with some wonder why it should be reckoned one of the world's seven wonders. There was the chaste Spanish Coronella committing her body to the devouring flames, rather than suffer her soul to flame with the least incentive or thought of lust. At the end of the hall in a large table, Cydias represented the Argonauts, for which Hortensius the Orator paid 144,000 sesterces. And next to that he showed us an original made by Pausias wherein his Glycera was represented, with a chaplet of flowers in her hand most elegantly plaited and twisted, the counterfeit of which for two talents of silver Lucius Lucullus bought of Dionysius, a painter of Athens. With these and divers others chaste and virtuous Dames was the hail furnished round, for other women living there were none, none being permitted to lodge in that holy court or to be there in the daytime, unless on certain festivals, when permitted, and that but seldom. After we had well viewed these chaste figures, we descended by some marble steps into another square court larger than the former, whose rich beauty exceeded the other, as much as the substance does the shadow. For the pavement was of precious chequered marble, the walls and windows all gilt, and in the midst stood an obelisk of one entire stone, half as high again as that which Sixtus Quintus caused to be translated from the Vatican, and now stands near St. Peter's Church in Rome; on this in lively figures were cut the perfect effigies of all the kings of that Island of Bensalem, and him you see standing on the top of all, said he, is the portrait of Altabin in corinthian metal and guilded; and this court, said he, in the Court Royal. Having viewed the glorious statues, in all their richly gilt caparisons, most of them being adorned with pearl and many precious stones, we passed through the glorious Temple of Good Works (whose walls engraved tell all the history of the Savior's works and passion) into the third quadrant. This is the imperial abode, said he, larger than any of the other courts. It was set with orange, lemon, pomegranate, and mulberry trees, and called the Court of Residence.

Hence we ascended by many stately black marble steps into the chamber of Presence, where Solomona was standing and conversing with his ancient and prime nobles, whom he familiarly called the Copartners of his care. With these he always conferred and maturely deliberated about all his civil affairs, it being his wonted saying (as I was after told) that it was much fitter

that he should embrace the faithful advice of
such and so many judicious friends (for so he
called all his counselors) than that they all
should follow and submit to his single will. He
was very plainly attired, as all his <u>nobles</u> were,
only distinguished by his brooch of diamonds and
rubies of the figure of a cross, on his miter-
like coronet; the rest of that Order of the <u>Holy</u>
<u>Cross</u> wearing theirs always at their breasts. He
was of middle stature, somewhat fair and ruddy,
and in whose mild and serene aspect might be
discovered those inward virtues and graces which
adorned his noble soul. For as <u>Joabin</u> then informed me, while he was busy in discourse, he was
the lively, exact exemplar of all princely virtues, in whom nothing was wanting that was requi-
site to make a prince both loved, feared, and
admired. His piety to God by his frequent addres-
ses to Him in his public and private devotion was
eminent. His indulgent love to his subjects, whom
he called his children, and his charity to re-
lieve the distressed was admirable. For those
subjects that decayed, he relieved; and where he
became heir to the goods and lands by treason
etc., he restored them to the children of the
deceased; if through misdemeanors they became
forfeit to him and the <u>Treasury of Charity</u>, he
either remitted his moiety to the delinquents or
gave it to the public treasury, it being his
usual saying that <u>kings that grow rich by the</u>
<u>spoil of their subjects seldom enjoy their own</u>
<u>with safety.</u> His <u>chastity</u> was singular, he being

never seen to converse with any woman but his
princely spouse or some of his nearest relations,
or lay with her after she proved pregnant, it
being his remark on unchaste livers that such as
did not reverence themselves would not reverence
God, whose image they bore. In his liberality he
was so beneficent that no deserving person ever
went from his presence unrewarded. To this purpose he erected Naon olergesigs, that temple so-
called and dedicated for the dispensing his good
deeds peculiarly, where once a day he constantly
distributed some doles, or honor, or advanced
some person, accounting (as Titus Vespasian did)
that day lost wherein he had not conferred some
benefit and good on somebody. In the search of
truth and humane learning, he was indefatigable,
allotting six hours every day to his studies. A
severe reprover of vice, he was frugal in his
expenses and very sparing in his diet. So abstem-
ious from any sort of liquor that between meals
he was seldom or never seen to drink so much as
water (which was his usual beverage, a little
sugared) and at meals but thrice, and then but
once of wine and water mixed. His clemency, man-
suetude, evenness of mind, constancy, courage,
and knowledge of the laws while he himself would
often sit in judicature were all wonderful, but
to enumerate all his princely endowments, said
he, as his strength of reason, memory and imagi-
nation, his profound skill in affairs of peace or
war, his subtle insight into men, as well as his
forts and havens, all which he knew so well he

could tell what ships they were capable of, where
situated, and with what winds to be entered, his
skill in tactics and all civil as well as mili-
tary exercises such as riding, running, wrest-
ling, vaulting, fencing, shooting, limming,*
etc., with many other delighted and excelled in,
the day would not be long enough to name them,
nor could I possibly set them all forth in their
native colors. At which pause of his I replied,
"<u>Oh</u> <u>how</u> <u>happy</u> <u>are</u> <u>the</u> <u>people</u> <u>that</u> <u>are</u> <u>governed</u> <u>by</u>
<u>such</u> <u>a</u> <u>prince,</u> <u>by</u> <u>whose</u> <u>efficacious</u> <u>example</u> <u>they</u>
<u>must</u> <u>needs</u> <u>be</u> <u>taught</u> <u>virtue</u>!" <u>Salomona</u> at that
instant casting his eyes round about espied us
being some ten in number, the rest stayed below;
and soon discovering us to be strangers, advanced
forward of his own accord to us, offering us his
stole, which as we each of us kneeled down to
kiss (as we had been instructed) he courteously
with his hand lifted each of us up again, and
lovingly embraced us, saying in the conclusion to
us all, "<u>Friends,</u> <u>you</u> <u>are</u> <u>espoused</u> <u>to</u> <u>this</u> <u>court</u>
<u>and</u> <u>kingdom,</u> <u>where</u> <u>you</u> <u>may</u> <u>live</u> as <u>freely</u> <u>as</u> <u>any</u>
<u>natural</u> <u>freeborn</u> <u>subjects</u> <u>I</u> <u>have.</u>" Hereat we all
bowed low, expressing our duties and thankfulness
in that submissive and silent posture. These
ceremonies performed, we retreated out of the
presence instantly (as <u>Joabin</u> had instructed us)
making three low obeisances as we receded still
backwards till we were out of it; none presuming

* To climb a rope beside a ladder.

there to turn the back parts to Majesty unless in the Church only.

He then carried us into the fourth court, equal to the rest in splendor and magnificence, in the midst of which under a high triumphal arch sustained by the <u>cardinal</u> virtues, were statues in brass, and those double gilt of the <u>twelve Apostles</u>, with descriptions on other pillars of their several martyrdoms. This was called the Court of Virtue. Having viewed this well, we passed through a stately hall into the <u>Academy</u> itself, to which it belonged. The <u>quadrangle</u> was envisioned on three sides with fair <u>cloisters</u>, the pillars and arches being of <u>mosaic</u>, of gold and azure and other curious colors, like that of Amarodoc at <u>Fez</u> in <u>Barbary</u>. "This is that eminent <u>Academy</u>," said he "...placed here in this glorious center for the concourse of all the prime selected wits throughout the nation, where they translate, write, license books, correct others, and purify the native language to the highest pitch of elegance. Right against the hall the library ranged, which was large and magnificent. Underneath it we passed into the fifth court, called the Court of <u>Orpheus</u>. In the midst of this, between several ranks of <u>laurel</u> and <u>myrtle</u> trees was a spacious fountain wherein <u>Orpheus</u> was playing on his harp, and ravishing with his divine melody (which by water was artificially made to resound) the approaching nymphs.

Thence he led us through an outward green court set with box, laurel, holly, ivy, fir, yew, cypress, juniper, tamarisk, rosemary, and many other sorts of green trees that with their verdure caused spring to dwell there all the year long, into a long paddock course, somewhat broader than ordinary, railed and set with firs and sycamores. About it multitudes of people were gathered, as well nobles as gentry, to behold the expected race. The race, soon after that Solomona was come, was thus performed: eight noblemen's jennets were placed in a rank at the farther end of the paddock, having no riders on them, only a few round, rattling bells were fastened to the saddle skirts, some of them made prickly so that, when they were all set forth on running together, these might spur them forward in the course. "This is our way of racing," said he "...performed without any danger or possibility of cheating in horsemanship, which is too often practiced by your European jockeys and riders." The race finished, the owner of the winning horse received the prize Solomona gave, which was a silver basin filled with 500 duckats in gold; the same horse being led away soon after with a garland on his head triumphantly and accompanied with divers sorts of loud and still music. In a large field, adjoining almost, in the midst thereof stood an amphitheater more famous than that Vespasian had begun at Rome and Titus finished. Here indeed many grave matrons, noble ladies, and beautiful young lasses with their beauties adorned the

theater, but their were all native and natural.
For here a painted face is looked on as a rotten
or painted post, and a patched one as beggarly.
For thus they argue the natural beauty best; if
the face be homely, say they, it is still God's
image, therefore lovely; if extraordinarily beautiful, the less reason by thinking to mend God's
workmanship to hide or disfigure any part of that
divine firmament.

Here the most excellent in their skill and
feats of activity from all parts of the nation
showed their cunning and dexterity. Some in <u>fenc-
ing,</u> <u>running,</u> <u>wrestling</u>, others in <u>shooting,</u>
<u>slinging,</u> <u>leaping,</u> <u>pitching</u> the <u>bar,</u> <u>vaulting,</u>
<u>darting</u> and other pastoral sports, where for all
that overcame were great rewards and prizes given
proportionably to the victors' deserts. But above
all the rest, <u>Solomona</u> seemed most to be taken
with one of the <u>Davidans</u>, or flingers of stones,
who not only outthrew all the rest, but directed
his charge so surely that he could hit the site
almost every time, and that with such a force
that the blow would prove as mortal as <u>David's</u>
did to great <u>Goliath.</u>

I then asked <u>Joabin</u> whether <u>Solomona</u> delighted not also in hunting now and then? To
which he answered negatively. "Not but that he
thinks the sport lawful," said he "...as it is
healthful for the body, but he accounts it loss
of precious time, and some kind of cruelty. Not

in the murder of any wild beasts (all as well
those of wild nature as other being alike subject
to man's dominion), but in the violent pursuit of
one of them to kill many good and serviceable
horses. Wherefore he permits it to the lusty
peasants only to destroy such as are most obnox-
ious, and can follow the chase on foot best,
supposing persons of quality and ennobled with
rich endowments of the mind, may better recreate
themselves in less tedious and toilsome pastimes.
And since most can shoot flying, the same dislike
he hath for hawking; for there they kill those
ravenous birds instead of maiming them. All games
at cards and dice are here discarded; only bowl-
ing and chess (which they play at as they ride),
because less provoking to passion, are generally
approved of. No pleasures but the most lawful and
innocent are liked of, it being a generally received maxim here, that all sensual pleasures are
brutish; accounting it the greatest pleasure upon
earth, next the serving of God, the doing of
kindnesses, and the pleasing remembrance of a
well acted life accompanied with the hopes of a
future fruition of a better." The day well nigh
spent in beholding these delightful sports (in
many of which Solomona himself contended with
some of his noblesse), he retired to his palace,
whither we attended him also to see his manner of
sitting at supper, and his attendance thereat;
which, so soon as he had visited the Temple, was
thus: his nobles according to their offices and
ranks brought in many silver dishes covered, and

presented them on a large <u>oval</u> <u>table</u> before him, about the midst of which he sat down so soon as the meat was blessed. But, as <u>Joabin</u> informed me, only two of those covered platters were lined with meat, and those but slight ones, of which also he ate but sparingly. Here were no <u>jestors</u> or <u>natural</u> <u>fools</u> about him, "to make his sauce pleasant with more saucy answers, as with you they are too usual," said <u>Joabin</u> "...in great men's houses. For the first here are looked on but as licensed knaves, the latter are pitied rather; and therefore kept private. For here it is as great a crime esteemed to mock a man for his weakness of mind as for his deformity of body, in neither of which he is to be blamed but pitied." In the space of one quarter of an hour or little more, the board and room was all cleared with great order and silence. His <u>nobles</u> and great <u>officers</u> ate immediately after altogether in the great hall. In this interval <u>Solomona</u> withdrew himself after his accustomed manner through a long privy gallery which led to his queen's court on the other side of the river, to visit her and his relations. The nobles, all dispatching their meal in as short a time, came up again attending his return which was not long after. After some discourses with the most eminent in their several sciences and professions, as occasion offered, he then withdrew wholly, appearing no more that night. Only he gave order to one as he went forth, that the <u>strangers</u>

should appear before him in the Temple of Good
Works the next morning.

We no sooner got back to the Stranger's
House, where after our wonted repast we sat ad-
miring the <u>virtues</u> and <u>glories</u> of the king of
<u>Bensalem</u>; but a <u>messenger</u> expressly brought the
summons, who making his address to us all, told
us it was, "His <u>Imperial</u> <u>Majesty's</u> <u>will</u> <u>and</u> <u>plea-</u>
<u>sure</u> <u>that</u> <u>all</u> <u>the</u> <u>strangers</u> <u>should</u> <u>appear</u> before
<u>him</u> <u>in</u> <u>the</u> Temple <u>of</u> <u>Good</u> <u>Works</u> <u>by</u> <u>eight</u> <u>of</u> <u>the</u>
<u>clock</u> <u>the</u> <u>next</u> morning; <u>that</u> <u>day</u> <u>being</u> <u>the</u> <u>holy</u>
<u>feast</u> <u>of</u> <u>St.</u> <u>Bartholomew.</u>" To this gracious sum-
mons I in the name of the rest, all likewise
bowing, told him, <u>that</u> <u>we</u> <u>were</u> <u>all</u> <u>prostrate</u> at
<u>the</u> <u>feet</u> <u>of</u> <u>his</u> <u>sovereign's</u> <u>princely</u> <u>devotion,</u>
<u>and</u> <u>should</u> <u>be</u> <u>ready</u> <u>to</u> <u>obey</u> <u>all</u> <u>his</u> <u>commands</u>,
thanking him particularly for his care and pains
in bearing that message. "It is but my duty,"
replied he "...I being the <u>superintendant</u> of the
ceremonies in that holy place. Therefore that you
may be preinstructed what is to be done there,
and how you are to behave yourselves, I shall a
little inform you. "At which courteous offer we
all bowed again, and showed a cheerful readiness
of attention. "My friends, you must then in brief
know," said he "that tomorrow is a general day of
healing the sick, of visiting others, and rewarding the poor, which our <u>Solomons</u> after himself
washing some of their feet, and his nobles the
rest, liberally performs. After these ceremonies
he installs three of his nobility, conferring on

them the high and sacred honor, or Order of the Holy Cross, there being never fewer than fifty of it and never above the number of threescore. Whilst those first rites are in performing, you are all to keep your stations, and on your knees except when Solomona will approach and reward you also. "Then assuring us he would himself place us there conveniently, he left us to our repose, and reminding us precisely of the hour, as not then to fail, he went his way.

The next morning we came at the appointed hour to the Temple of Good Works, where the superintendant courteously received us, and placed us all in three rows in a corner thereof by ourselves. Here so soon as divine service was ended, Solomona descended from his imperial chair, and walking about the temple ministered to everyone's necessity, as he was on his bare knees in order placed, and as his particular wants required. Some he touched and praying over them healed them, for (as Joabin had informed me) he had the gift of healing also, as some of your European kings have, particularly those of England from Edward the confessor's time, and those of France. He washed the wounds of others, and of others he anointed their sores; and to all he gave some money or largess. While this was in performing, Joabin (who knelt by us) informed me; how that the temple ceremonies all being ended, not only these but many other poor and aged persons were to be feasted in the great hall, where <u>Solomona</u> before they sat down used to wash the feet of some, and give new raiment to others. And that so soon as they had dined, we were also there to be feasted.

    This Ceremony of the <u>Doles</u> being ended, the other of the installments of the three nobles into the Order of the Holy Cross began. They were clad in long, sad* russet coats made of <u>camel's</u> hair, having loose and wide sleeves, and turned up with white flannel, tied only close about the middle with a white silken girdle also, in token of their innocence. Each of them had on his right shoulder a long wooden cross, as long and heavy as that of the <u>Cyrenians</u>. Laden with these, and conducted by the <u>superintendant</u> one after the other, in a slow pace and humble posture, they first presented themselves with their offerings of gold at the high altar; and then soon after, according to <u>Solomona's</u> example, all the rest of the Order did the like. Here having made their orations, <u>Solomona</u> first making three bows and the rest doing the like, all but the three that were to be installed returned to their several cells, where they sat still for half an hour during which time the <u>Temple</u> and <u>choir</u> echoed with most ravishing and heavenly music. The melody ended, the <u>Superintendant</u> went up to the holy altar (before which the three <u>nobles</u> were all this while on their bare knees) and conducted

* Dark-colored

them with their crosses on their shoulders to the imperial chair. Here each of them in order laying down his holy burden, and kneeling between <u>Solomona's</u> knees, he with his hand on the <u>Croisodan's</u> head blessed each of them severally, saying, "<u>God bless you, Soldier, and make you a faithful son of the Church Militant and constant follower of the Savior.</u>"

So soon as he had thus severally blessed them all, he gave to each of the three new <u>Croisodans</u> (so those knights were ever after called) a gilt sword, which he girded about their loins, and charged them to draw only in defense of the Christian faith. After that he gave to each of these three a cross of <u>diamonds</u> and <u>rubies</u>, in exchange for the wooden ones, which as trophies of their honor were to be left and laid in the Temple. This fastened to a red ribbon he hung about each of their necks and, as he so did, charged him he should always wear it at his breast in token of his hearty and ready obedience to take up the other again whensoever the Savior, the ever blessed <u>General</u> of that Order, should require. Dismissed with this charge, or oath of <u>fidelity</u> (for other oath the subject of <u>Bensalem</u> takes none, as knowing that all that be Christ's followers will be obedient and faithful to his Anointed Vice-regent), they were forthwith by the <u>Superintendant</u> proclaimed <u>Croisodans</u> and <u>Christian defenders</u> or the <u>Holy Cross</u>. Immediately after this proclamation they retired into a little vestry, whence they came forth apparalled in most glorious vestments, and were then conducted to their particular cells on high amongst the rest of that noble Order. Then after a To God was sung, all solemnly standing up with their faces to the East, with great variety of sweet voices and musical instruments, they all with their swords drawn in their right hands made a public confession of their faith. After all these hymns and ceremonies thus decently performed, Solomona (unto whom all both himself and they had offered, was brought, their offerings being very large, those installation days especially) descended and distributed them amongst us the Strangers, each of our shares amounting to no less than two hundred duckats. For the whole offering he had before appointed to be divided equally, and put into so many crimson silk purses as we were strangers, which he distributed amongst us, giving to each of us one. After this the music ceased, and he proclaimed his general pardon to all offenders against law and justice, all whom once in twelve years (as Joabin told me) were at this festival usually released, pardoned, and enlarged; concluding all at his exit with this holy and heavenly prayer:

"May God so forgive me and all the world."

Which said, he went out first himself, the Croisodans following next, and then the other

lords, gentry, and people in quiet order while
all the choristers sung this anthem:

"Praise, honor and glory is owed to God,
the best and the greatest onto
centuries of centuries.
Amen."

APPENDIX

Due to the fact that the modern printing of this book has a different pagination, we have reproduced all the pages involved in paging errors. This is for the convenience of students who may be concerned with a special meaning for these so-called errors which do coincide with an esoteric ritual set forth in the original book.

53   *The New Atlantis.*

is useful to mankind, either at home by rewarding them with great Pensions, or from abroad by erecting their statues.

WE study the publick good so much, that whereas we reward those that discover, so he is in some measure punished that conceals and hides a benefit which may pleasure his countrey: For they that do no good when they can, as well as they that do mischief are here accounted debtors alike, and are looked on as unnatural children to their Common parent their Countrey.

THis said, he offered me the view of their *Codes* and *Presidents*, if at any time I pleased to come to the Seminary of *Law-Students* to be farther instructed in their laws and form of Government. Here I rising up made a low obeysance, and kissed the hem of his tippet again: giving him many & large thanks for the favour he had already done me, in imparting to me so many wholesom laws and divine constitutions. And though he seemed willing to enlarge the conference at that time, wishing me to sit down again by him: yet to prevent me of that happiness in came immediately a messenger with a red tip-staff gilt at both ends, in his hand, & whispered him away about some urgent affairs. Whereupon troubled a little to leave me so abruptly, he turned to me, & said, *My Friend, at this time I must a sk your pardon, being commanded hence in hast: to morrow*

The New Atlantis.   54.

row or any day next week if you please to see our Seminary, I shall be at more leisure, and glad to enlarge my self farther to you. So he left me, and as he went out caused the delinquent to be taken forth the Pillory: whence descending he fell down upon his bare knees, and asked the *Alcaldorem* and all Christian People, whom he had by his ill example offended, forgiveness. This done, and the Judge forgiving him; and giving him a short monitory charge, he went about his affa rs; whilst the poor Offendour was led away to receive the other part of his punishment.

The next day my intended visit to the *Alcaldorem* was prevented, for *Joabin* came that morning early to see me, and told us (Sirs) you are like to be enriched three dayes hence at the next City about two Karans and a half of with the Regalio of as pleasing an entertainment, and specious shew, as I believe your eyes have ever beheld. For the ingenious *Verdugo* (so was he called) that hath of late found out the way of making Linnen cloath, and consequently paper of *Asbestinum* or *Linum vivum* that fire shall not consume the writing (which paper is called *Salamandrian*) by the help of some mineral powders and the Spirit of Vitriol, is, being born and bred there, for this his rare invention, now there to be honoured by the chief of all the City and province, and after a great Feast and other ceremonies and pastimes, to receive his reward. This according to the Custom is

E 4   al-

No. 1: This is the second page numbered 53. 54 follows naturally. There is no page 55.

56   *The New Atlantis.*

alwaies made proportionable to the worth of the invention and the merits of the perfon, I fhall therefore (faid he) provide a conveni- ent place for you and your fellows, where you fhall all fee his graceful entrie into the the City, and entertainment afterwards at the great Hall of *Solomons* Houfe; where I will al- fo provide for you a ftanding to behold the *Triumphs,* to hear the fpeech which is to be expreffed in the Spanifh tongue, as alfo a paftoral enterlude. We all thanked him for this his noble offer, being exceeding joyful at the news. The præfixed day being come, conducted by him we all got thither betimes on Mules he provided, and took our ftands near the Gate St. *Mark* (the Gates there ta- king their names from the Churches they ftand next to) where all the Nobles, Magi- ftrates and chief Citizens fplendidly equipped met *Verdugo* on Horfeback, and welcomed him at his firft entry.

He was a middle-fized man, of a fprightlie mien and ingenuous countenance, difcover- ing in his bold afpeft a fubtile vivacity and promptnefs to undertake and perform great things. Here appeared forty proper men on Horfeback, all clad in crimfon fatten loofe coats. Immediately after them and before *Verdugos* chariot, a ftately *Pageant* no lefs glorious then the other, was drawn with fower black horfes a breaft, richly trapped and plumed, wherein on an imperial throne, a fair youth, perfonating *Minerva* the Goddefs of

The New Atlantis.   57

of Invention was feated, holding forth in her right hand a rowle of Paper, fired at both ends, as who would fay, lighting *Verdugo* to his crown of Glory. This emblem (as he told me) is ever varied according to the prefent invention. *Verdugo* followed mounted on a high Triumphal *Chariot* of gilt *Cedar,* drawn by fower milke white *Jennets* a breaft, and thofe trapped with fcarlet and filver-embroy- dered velvet. His veftment was like himfelf, youthful both for fafhion, garb, and colour, being of a graffegreen fattin, made clofe to the body, and over it a mantle of the fame richly embroydered, and lined with cloth of filver, carelefly hanging over one fhoulder. On his head he wore a light gold Laurel ena- meld with green: through which his auburn locks, both long and curling, did burnifh and fhine like fo many funbeams. By his fide he wore a filver hilted fword, tyed in a fair crim- fon taffata embroidered fcarf: which wea- pon (as *Joabin* told me) was only permitted to thefe triumphant inventours to wear ever after in the City, to maintain and vindicate themfelves the fole Authors of that their in- vention againft all counterfeit pretenders or gainfaying oppofers. To this end he wore a bright gantlet alfo on his right hand inftead of his glove: the other being carried by one on horfeback immediately before him. Clofe behind his Chariot attended the *Nobles, Ma- giftrates, Gentry* and *Citizens,* two and two; the chief on horfeback, the reft on foot: the ftreets

No. 2: Pages 56 and 57 follow in proper order.

125

62   The New Atlantis.

ſtreets and windows (which were richly carpetted) being thronged with orderly and ſi-
lent Spectators. Whilſt they all advanced
thus towards the great Hall, this firſt part of
the ſhow being paſt, the Jew haſtily conducted us a back way to the Palace, that we might
there be ſeated before the reſt came, to prevent the preſſe of People that flocked thither
as it were to ſome Coronation. As ſoon as
Verdugo came into the great Court before the
Hall (which ecchoed with Trumpets and o-
ther loud inſtruments) they all lighted from
their horſes attending Verdugo on foot; who
then alighted alſo from his Chariot; and at
his entrance into the hall was embraced with
both arms,(by that ſame Father that before
had given me his bleſſing) and who there
ſtood with the Fraternity of the Houſe ready
to receive him. Cloſe by him one of the
chief and moſt eloquent Brethren did there
deliver a moſt elegant ſpeech. The effect of
it was the commendation of Learning in general; with a particular Encomium of that
his late invention, extolling the admirable
ingenuity thereof for the perpetual advance
of Learning,with a full exemplification of the
good and benefit that did indubitably accrue not to themſelves only but to all poſterity, and concluding with great thanks to the
happy inventour of that noble Art, and
praiſes to God the enleightner of our under-
ſtandings, and ſole Author and Giver of all
good things. This gratulatory Eulogium being

The New Atlantis.   63

ing finiſhed, the Father of Solomons houſe took
off his green upper mantle, and inveſted him
with Minervas long Robe, which was a ſtole
down to the ground, richly embroidered of
gold,ſilk and ſilver flowers in needle work.
Minerva then took off his former Laurel, and
placed her own Garland upon his head, which
was moſt elegant for compoſure, adorned
with all the variety of the choiceſt flowers ex-
preſſed in their proper native colours, and to
the life ſhadowed forth in ſilk, gold and ſilver.
Over it was ſuperadded a Crown of divers
raies, in each of which in fine ingravery the
names of all the moſt ingenious Authors and
Inventours ſince our firſt Altabins time (who
was the firſt King of this Iſland) were curiouſ-
ly inſerted. This done, the Father laying
his right hand bare upon his head bleſſed him
(as he was preſented to him on his knees by
Minerva) ſaying: God bleſſe thee, my Son, and
enlighten thy great underſtanding more and
more, for the benefit of mankind and this our
Iſland of Benſalem. We admit you now as fellow, Brother and Companion into this our Socie-
tie. Here Verdugo having bowed and kiſſed
the verge of his Tippet, the Father lifted him
up with his right hand, and fixed him on his
legs again: And immediately preſented him
with a great ſilver Baſon full charged with
5000. Duckats in Gold, declaring farther
that beſides that gratuity from the Society,
the State was pleaſed to reward his great de-
ſerts with the yearly penſion of 5000 Duckats
more

No. 3: Pages numbered 62 and 63 follow 57.

60   *The New Atlantis.*

more to him and his Poſterity. Thereupon he requeſted him to declare his invention,with the true manner of effecting it, according to cuſtome,for the public good of the ſtate and benefit of mankind. The reaſon of this their cuſtom (as *Joabin* told me) was not ſo much to prevent *Monopolizing* or ingroſſing that beneficial commodity to himſelf,wherby he only might vend his bad wares (which would be but the enriching of one man to beggar many) but chiefly to inſtruct others alſo in it, that the Invention ſhould not periſh with the Author; and be rather meliorated and augmented by the æmulous wits of Ingenious imitatours. Then after he had preſented to him in writing the Schedule of tho true manner of perfecting that work , the Father did take him by the left hand and *Minerva* by the right,leading him thus betwixt them into the next great room (which was richly hung and carpetted, and where he was ſumptuouſly feaſted ; all the houſe in the interim ecchoing with variety of ſweet muſick, ſometimes ſtill, otherwiſe loud, ſometimes reſounding with joyfull acclamations, and ſometimes again with ſoft melodious ſongs,the firſt proclaiming,the laſt whiſpering the praiſes,worth and merits of the ever famed *Verdugo.*

Whilſt they were feaſting within, *Joabin* told me, that ſo ſoon as dinner was ended, the *Father* was to record the invention in a book of that *Salamandrian* paper *Verdugo* had preſen-

The New Atlantis.   61

ſented them; with his the Authors name and Sirname,and place of birth, and the true manner of effecting it, the inventour himſelf being by, to atteſt it his invention under his own hand. This book of Regiſter(ſaid he) is carefully there to be preſerved in *Solomons* Houſe to all perpetuity. Then leading me into a long and large Gallery by the Hall, he ſhewed me the ſtatues of all the prime inventours in many ages before, wherewith that ſpatious room was above almoſt furniſhed round. Amongſt the reſt he firſt pointed out the inventour of Paper, whoſe name (as he there ſhewed it me under written)was *Papyrius,* whence it took it firſt denomination ; and not from the *Ægyptian Papyri* or ſedgy weeds they firſt uſed (as you *Europæans,* ſaid he, conjecturally ſuppoſe) being preſt into thin flakes or leaves, and dryed,to write on. For this ſame *Papyrius* (he added) firſt invented our paper made with rags in King *Ptolomies* time,a little before he raiſed his famous Library at *Alexandria.* Then he ſhewed me the Effigies in tranſparent ' Chriſtall of the unfortunate inventour of *Vitrum ductile* or malleable glaſs, whoſe invention *Tiberius* rewarded with death, and juſt underneath it this *Epitaph* written,

Qui vitro & ſibi vitam dedit,electro velut
Apes incluſa & perlucidior ſuo,
Monumentum glaciavit hoc ære perennius,
        Faber.

                        Quem

No. 4: Pages 60 and 61 follow 62 and 63.

57 *The New Atlantis.*

Quem dum vitreum enecavit Tiberius,
Inventum non potis erat egelidare.

Next to that was the Pourtrait of him that firſt invented the *Pixis nautica* or Sea-card to ſail by with; and this *Encomium* of the perſon under it,

Acum qui tetigit, & acus indicavit uſum,
Terra di Lavoro oriundus, & natare te docens,
Ipſe ſtat in cælis
Septentrio,
Flavius.

Then he pointed to me the ingenious Inventour of preſerving Gunpowder from taking fire, by which preſervative art, learnt probably from hence, the *Venetian Arſenals*, *Magazins*, and Cities are preſerved from ruine, under which to the eternal memory of the Authour I read theſe fower lines,

Ignem è cælo ſuffuratus eſt Prometheus ;
Hic alter è pulvere nitrato, Sulphur ;
Gaſparus Botallus: Oh divina Furta !
Quæ ſalvos interim nos eſſe juſſitant !

Cloſe by him was the pourtrait of *Magellanus* his ſhip, called the Victory, ſailing, and of himſelf on the upper deck of it : and underneath it theſe verſes inſcribed,

Prima

The New Atlantis. 58

Prima ego velivolis ambivi curſibus orbem,
Magellane, novo te duce ducta freto ;
Ambivi, meritoque vocor Victoria ; nunc mi
Vela ale, pretium gloria, pugna mare

And next by him he ſhewed me with a certain Aſteriſm of high remarque, the bold Sr. *Fraucis Drake*, pictured alſo ſailing on a little globe ; who next after *Magellanus*, he told me, girdled the world, with theſe verſes underwritten,

Drake, pererrati novit quem terminus orbis,
Quemque ſemel mundi vidit uterque polus :
Si taceant homines, facient te ſidera notum ;
Sol neſcit comitis non memor eſſe ſui.

Almoſt next to this he ſhewed me the ingenious phanſie of the Painter *Palaton*, who had pourtraied *Homer* that Prince of Poets vomiting, and all the reſt of them licking it up, with this Diſtic writ underneath it,

Adspice Mæoniden, a quo ceu fonte perenni,
Vatum Pieriis ora rigantur aquis.

Cloſe to this ſtood that elaborate and moſt incentive piece of *Venus*, which *Praxiteles* drew ſo to the life that a young man fell in love with it ; with this diſtic under it,

Ixion nubem, Juveniſque hanc deperit umbram:
Non tamen hæc Divæ eſt umbra, ſed ipſa Venus.
By

No. 5: Pages 57 and 58 follow pages 60 and 61.

79 *The New Atlantis.*

ed for Morning no sooner appeared, but *Jo-abin* accompanied with thirteen Carrioles desired that the whole company would be spectators of that solemn festivity, to which purpose he had brought (he said) Carrioles enough and those convenient for us all. His importunity would not admit of any denyal, so that we all ascended into them as he had ordered our places, & advanced somewhat before sunrise. Sometimes drawn by land, and otherwhiles at certain stages by water, that evening we arrived at a convenient *Vento* or Inn in the midway, where we had all conveniencies and respect imaginable. besides our entertainment, which was *Gratis* to us Strangers only. The next morning we again prevented the sun by our early advance, in regard we were to reach the Court that day, which we did in good time with much ease and pleasure. But by the Way a little before noon we entred one of the three Universities, wherein was the most famous Colledg of *Agriculture* that the Island afforded. Here after we had refreshed our selves, to pass away two or three howers of the hottest part of the day, he brought me acquainted with the *Providoran General* and Principle then of that famous Colledge. A reverend old man he was, and no less learned in the history of nature, then full of curteous humanity both in his discourse and carriage. He first led us into a very fair physic Garden, wherein he told us were almost as many medecinable

The New Atlantis. *78*

its decent bravery, curious sculptures, and rare antiquities, with its library (which each Church, he told me, there had one) he returned home with me, and by the way informed me of a splendid appearance *Solomona* was to make in public the third day after, upon accasion of a great horse-race with other innocent pastimes wherewith the people entertained the King that whole day. Now if your self (said he) or as many as will of your company, please to go to the Imperial City, you shall ride thitherward to morrow morning, and their I shall use the means that you shall not only kisse our *Solomonoaes* stole, but behold the gaities and solemnities of that grand appearance, with the modest port and quiet government of that glorious Court, and the magnificent *Structures* thereof.

Hereat having anticipated these future prospects by a right supposal of their transcendent excellencies beyond all we had yet seen, I accepted of his kind offer with great joy and alacrity, and told him, that since he was pleased to undertake the trouble, we would all attend him that voyage at the day. *Joabin* then taking his leave at the door of the Strangers house, whither his civility had returned me, willed me and the rest of our company that designed that voyage (which he hoped would be all) to be ready in our best Equipage very early next morning, when he would not fail to be with us. The wished

No. 6: Pages 79 and 78 numbers should be reversed.